W9-AAE-406

JESUS,
LOVER
OF A
WOMAN'S
SOUL

JESUS
Lover
OF A
WOMAN'S SOUL

ERWIN & REBECCA LUTZER

TYNDALE HOUSE PUBLISHERS, INC
CAROL STREAM, ILLINOIS

Visit Tyndale's exciting Web site at www.tyndale.com

TYNDALE is a registered trademark of Tyndale House Publishers, Inc.

Tyndale's quill logo is a trademark of Tyndale House Publishers, Inc.

Jesus, Lover of a Woman's Soul

Copyright © 2006 by Erwin and Rebecca Lutzer. All rights reserved.

Cover art courtesy of Musee des Beaux-Arts, Reims, France/J.P. Zenobel/Bridgeman Art Library. All rights reserved.

Author photo copyright © by Jim Whitmer Photography. All rights reserved.

Back cover photograph of floor © by iStockphoto.com. All rights reserved.

Designed by Beth Sparkman

Scripture quotations marked NIV are taken from the *Holy Bible,* New International Version®. NIV®. Copyright © 1973, 1978, 1984 by International Bible Society. Used by permission of Zondervan. All rights reserved.

Scripture quotations marked KJV are taken from the *Holy Bible,* King James Version.

Scripture quotations marked NASB are taken from the *New American Standard Bible, ©* 1960, 1962, 1963, 1968, 1971, 1972, 1973, 1975, 1977 by The Lockman Foundation. Used by permission.

Scripture quotations marked (ESV) are from *The Holy Bible,* English Standard Version, copyright © 2001 by Crossway Bibles, a division of Good News Publishers. Used by permission. All rights reserved.

Scripture taken from the New King James Version. Copyright © 1979, 1980, 1982 by Thomas Nelson, Inc. Used by permission. All rights reserved.

Library of Congress Cataloging-in-Publication Data

Lutzer, Erwin W.
  Jesus, lover of a woman's soul / Erwin and Rebecca Lutzer.
    p. cm.
Includes bibliographical references and index.
ISBN-13: 978-0-8423-8426-1 (hc : alk. paper)
ISBN-10: 0-8423-8426-X (hc : alk. paper)
ISBN-13: 978-0-8423-8427-8 (sc : alk. paper)
ISBN-10: 0-8423-8427-8 (sc : alk. paper)
1. Jesus Christ—Views on women. 2. Women in the Bible. 3. Bible. N.T. Gospels—Criticism, interpretation, etc. I. Lutzer, Rebecca. II. Title.
  BT590.W6L88 2006
  232.90082—dc22   2005030828

Printed in the United States of America

11   10   09   08   07   06
 6   5   4   3   2   1

To our lovely daughters
Lorisa, Lynette, Lisa,
women of faith and hope
who know that Jesus loves them.
They have brought us much joy,
taught us many things,
and given us darling grandchildren.

CONTENTS

ACKNOWLEDGMENTS

We want to express our deepest thanks to the wonderful team at Tyndale House Publishers. Their warmth and expertise guided us to write passionately about Jesus, and compassionately for all the women who will read this book.

Jan Long Harris
Sharon Leavitt
Nancy Clausen
Caleb Sjogren
Lisa Jackson
Bonne Steffen

Jan, as associate publisher, you challenged and inspired us to write the book. Lisa, as senior editor, you guided and labored with us. It was a pleasure to work with you.

Thank you to the wonderful staff at The Lodge in Buchanan, Michigan, who extended the most generous hospitality to us as we meditated on the Scriptures and worked on the manuscript. We will always be grateful for your kindness.

Finally, thank you to the dear women whose gripping stories became a part of this book. We pray that your trials and suffering will be used by God to encourage and inspire other women who even now seek Jesus, the lover of their souls.

Erwin and Rebecca Lutzer

INTRODUCTION

JESUS AND TODAY'S WOMAN

What relevance does a man who lived two thousand years ago have for today's woman? If that man is Jesus, the answer—in a single word—*plenty!*

Today Jesus reaches to us across the centuries, inviting us to come to Him for the same hope and healing He gave to the women He encountered so long ago. Unlike other great teachers, who can only inspire us by their example, Jesus still connects with us, asking that we respond to His invitation of restoration and personal validation. His promises of rest for the weary, bread for the spiritually hungry, and forgiveness for the guilty are just as valid today as when He first made them.

"Jesus was the original feminist," the fictional character Sir Leigh Teabing explains to cryptologist Sophie Neveu in the novel *The Da Vinci Code*.[1] For many people, the word *feminist* conjures up images of radical individualism, abortion rights, and a host of other "causes." We can say with confidence that Jesus was not a feminist in this modern sense. Nor did He intend that the church be built on Mary Magdalene, as author Dan Brown claims in his mega–best seller.

If by *feminist* we mean that Jesus broke with the demeaning view the men of His day had of women; if we mean that He overstepped the legalistic boundaries of prejudice—if such be our interpretation of the phrase, then *yes*, Jesus was "the original feminist." Jesus *was* revolutionary in His treatment of women. He dared to believe in the ministry of women and valued them in a way that was foreign to His times.

Today, critics tell us that Christianity has encouraged a male-dominated, women-suppressing culture. It is quite true that women have often been treated as second-class citizens throughout the history of the church, and plenty of derogatory remarks about them can be produced to support the claim. But such a bias against women cannot be traced to the pages of the New Testament or the early church. In the first centuries after Jesus' death and resurrection, for the most part, women who were followers of Jesus were honored, and their husbands in turn were taught to honor their wives. Many of the strictures that later Christian writers placed on women have more to do with popular culture than with the New Testament itself.

In this book, we intend to show how Jesus undercut the double standard that marginalized women in His day. In doing so, He did not negate the teachings of the Old Testament, but rather, He revealed that the religious leaders had added their own self-righteous restrictions to the Law and ignored the totality of its teaching. Unfortunately, these religious leaders merged the customs of the day with their own personal bias and elevated these to divine status. Jesus affirmed and validated women as equal partners in the family of God, which He came to establish. When He proclaimed liberty to the captives, He did so, in part, by countering the debilitating cultural bias against women. Jesus clearly created a new family of brothers and sisters who shared the same heavenly Father (Mark 3:31-35). Thus, as members of the new family, women must have equality of spiritual privilege.

Jesus made no explicit comments about changing the Old Testament order of male leadership in worship and within the family structure. He even chose twelve male apostles. But in His personal dealings, He simply ignored the prevalent traditions of His day, traditions that relegated women to a second-class status. In His presence, women came out of hiding and were validated as daughters of God.

Many of you know the stories of the men who left all to follow Jesus. But we often overlook the women who also left all to follow Him. We can only appreciate such a radical idea when we realize that Jewish women of that day were not even supposed to read the Scriptures, much less leave their homes, except briefly to fulfill a domestic responsibility. A first century rabbi went so far as to say that the words of the Torah (the Hebrew Scripture) should be burned rather than be entrusted to a woman. And yet, Jesus shared His Word with many different women as He walked the dusty roads of ancient Israel. In fact, He entrusted the most important message of the early church—that of His own resurrection—to be first proclaimed by a woman with a dubious past.

In short, the purpose of this book is to lead you into the heart of Jesus. You will see how He broke many taboos, how He rejected the entrenched stereotypes, and how He was willing to be misunderstood in order to help the women He encountered.

If you could meet Jesus today, what would your request be?

Forgiveness?

Healing?

Eternal life?

Deliverance?

Cleansing?

Validation?

Hope?

Love?

The women who met Jesus had the same needs. Some of them sought Him out, while others were found by Him. Each had exhausted human resources, and all needed a miracle from someone who understood them and would not condemn them. Some had great faith; others did not.

Every story in this book tells of a divine encounter. And you can meet the same Jesus today if you come to Him with your deepest longings. He calls out to us today in a voice loud enough to be heard amid the din of our gender-biased culture.

Our prayer is that when you are finished reading these chapters, you will be able to say with deep confidence *Jesus is the lover of my soul*.

Join us on a journey that points the way.

Erwin and Rebecca Lutzer
Moody Church
Chicago, Illinois

After this, Jesus traveled about from one town and village to another, proclaiming the good news of the kingdom of God. The Twelve were with him, and also some women who had been cured of evil spirits and diseases: Mary (called Magdalene) from whom seven demons had come out; Joanna the wife of Cuza, the manager of Herod's household; Susanna; and many others. These women were helping to support them out of their own means. LUKE 8:1-3

1

JESUS, LOVER OF
MARY MAGDALENE

Karla entered our lives in the early years of our ministry. Childhood trauma had left Karla unsure of how to cope with the challenges and stresses of living in the real world. She was young, an immature Christian, and had been going through emotional and spiritual turmoil for several months. Her two-year marriage was challenging, and her job was stressful and mentally demanding.

Added to these situations was the burden of her invalid mother, who frequently relied on Karla to care for her physical and emotional needs. Many years before, her mother had left a major religious cult, and she still struggled occasionally with frightening visions and evil oppression. She had recently shared with Karla that she had a trancelike dream of evil images that had terrified her, and that she remembered calling out over and over again for Karla.

As the confusion and tension grew inside her mind, Karla began to have unusual and scary thoughts herself. One day while at work she shared her fears with a coworker, an overzealous believer from a different religious group. Over the lunch hour, the woman insisted upon laying hands on her and praying in an unusual manner.

Within a short time, Karla began to hear voices. Her perception of reality started changing, and she began to have grandiose thoughts about herself.

Later that same day, in an altered state of consciousness, Karla left her job and drove to her neighborhood. Going from door to door, she made bizarre pronouncements about Jesus and the end of the world. She even stopped at a playground to warn the children of impending doom. Concerned about her behavior, one of the neighbors called the police. Even after her husband arrived, Karla was uncooperative.

Her husband decided to take her to the hospital for evaluation. While there, she told the medical staff that she had the power of Jesus. When she began demonstrating unusual strength, she was forcibly restrained and sedated with psychiatric drugs designed to put her in a state of artificial calmness.

This is where we entered the picture. After receiving a phone call about this situation, we began to prayerfully intercede for this desperate young woman. Within the hour, Karla became peaceful and spoke rationally, and the next day she was released from the hospital. The doctor said that she had suffered a nervous breakdown and told her to rest and to take tranquilizers. She remained rational, but her inner turmoil continued.

I (Rebecca) was able to meet with Karla soon after her release. For several hours, God gave me the compassion and patience to listen and to talk with her. Her thoughts were confused and unfocused. What she knew about herself, her life, and her relationship with God were in conflict. At times, she was agitated; occasionally, she cried inconsolably. I believed that she was under demonic oppression. With her permission, in the name of Jesus, I spoke directly to the evil spirits that were torturing her, commanding them to stop and to leave her presence. After this, her countenance relaxed; she became calm and began to concentrate and to understand the spiritual battle that she was going through.

We believed Karla needed a safe, quiet place in which to recover; a place where she could receive counseling and help in a concentrated effort to restore her peace of mind. It was very important for her to know that she could be delivered from all demonic influence and oppression. We discussed Karla's experience with a pastor friend who had written a book about spiritual warfare. He concluded that some of the demonic spirits that had been tormenting Karla's mother had transferred to Karla. We were willing to commit whatever time and effort it would take to see full deliverance and restoration for Karla. Though we were new at dealing with cases like this, we were eager to learn how to fight against demonic spirits. We invited her to stay with us.

Karla was childlike in her thinking and responses. Her concept of who she was in Christ had been shattered. Thoughts of despair and suicide troubled her. She had believed the lies of Satan rather than the truth of Scripture. Through prayer and reading and studying the Bible, God enabled us to guide her back to biblical truth and a "sound mind." As we listened to her and showed gentle, patient love, the Holy Spirit began the healing process of restoring her soul.

We have kept in touch with Karla throughout the years. Her life has not been easy—she's struggled with an unfaithful husband, divorce, single parenting, financial difficulties, health problems, and being misunderstood by others. But she has never wavered in her faith in Jesus, who became the lover of her soul. Just as Jesus delivered Mary Magdalene from her tormenting demons, He also did the same for Karla. And just as Mary Magdalene devoted her life to following Jesus, loving Him more than any other person, so has Karla. Jesus did for them what no one else could—He forgave their sins, delivered them, made them whole, and restored their sanity—is it any wonder that they love Him so?

ᎧᎯ

One of the best-kept secrets is the role that women played in the early church. And today no woman is receiving more attention than Mary Magdalene.

She is deserving of renewed interest and study. For many centuries she was dismissed as the "penitent prostitute" who interrupted a feast in the house of a Pharisee to show her devotion to Christ. To be sure, the official church was glad she received forgiveness, but the accusation stigmatized her as a woman of the streets. She was grudgingly praised for introducing herself to Christ, but she could not escape the disgrace of the scarlet letter.

This misidentification can be traced back to AD 591 when Pope Gregory gave a message in which he said that the prostitute whose story is recorded in Luke 7 was really Mary Magdalene who was mentioned in Luke 8 as the woman delivered from possession by seven devils. However, scholars agree that there was no reason to make such a connection. In Luke's Gospel the story of the unnamed prostitute is separate from the later reference to Mary Magdalene. Not until the Second Vatican Council in 1964 did the Catholic Church officially correct the error.

Read Luke 8:1-3 and you will agree that the author introduces Mary Magdalene as a new person in the life of Jesus. No effort is made to connect her with the previous story about the woman who anointed Jesus at the feast in Simon's house. Yes, Mary was a troubled woman before she met Jesus, but we have no reason to think that she was a harlot.

Mary Magdalene has come to symbolize the struggle of women throughout the centuries: often misunderstood, casually dismissed, and eclipsed by the role men play in spiritual leadership. This woman who occupied a prominent place in Jesus' life has too often been stigmatized by a church dominated by male leadership that has, at best, grudgingly recognized the contribution women have made to the history of the Christian faith.

Mary Magdalene has many sisters. She provides motivation for all the women who sit in the pews of our churches, desiring an opportunity to serve but unsure whether they will be accepted and affirmed. Many gifted women seek in vain to be validated, to feel useful and respected in meaningful ministry. The story of Mary, whose life began in secret turmoil and ended with a personal affirmation from Jesus, gives us all hope. This woman with a troubled past ended up being the first witness to the resurrection of her Lord.

In the final chapter of this book, we shall discuss the contemporary debate about Mary Magdalene as she is depicted in the Gnostic Gospels and in the novel *The Da Vinci Code*. We will answer questions about her relationship to the Holy Grail and French royalty. But in the rest of this chapter we will study her place in the New Testament by examining several snapshots of her relationship with Jesus.

TRANSFORMED BY JESUS

Jesus did what no rabbi of His day would ever have approved: He allowed women to travel with Him on His journeys throughout Israel. One of those followers was Mary Magdalene, a woman who evidently was unmarried since she was identified only by where she came from. The name Magdalene, or Magdala, probably refers to modern day Migdal, which historically has been an important agricultural, fishing, and trade center on the western shore of ancient Galilee.

We don't know where Mary and Jesus first met. Perhaps it was when He visited her town near Galilee. She had heard about His miracles and sought deliverance through His healing power.

Mary Magdalene's distinguishing characteristic is that she underwent an exorcism at the command of Jesus. She was possessed by evil spirits, who no doubt terrorized her. There has been much speculation regarding the seven demons Mary is said to have had. The fourteenth-century Italian poet Dante believed Mary Magdalene's demons were not literal; he termed them as seven scars: pride, envy, anger, intemperance, lasciviousness (lust or salaciousness), covetousness, and spiritual sloth.

Actually, Dante might well have underplayed Mary's predicament. Passages in the New Testament that speak about demons should not be interpreted as superstitions of an ancient era; nor are they symbolic references to psychological scars. The record shows that Jesus often encountered alien spirits who had an independent existence and tried to defy Jesus' authority, even speaking to Him at times. In this case, we know that when Mary Magdalene met Jesus, He delivered her from their power.

Those of us interested in the underlying causes of human behavior would like to sit down with Mary and ask about her past. We'd like to know when she became aware of these alien spirits, and how she coped with her suffering. Was she involved in occult practices?

Of course, we don't know the answers to these questions. But we do know something of the common characteristics of those who are haunted by unseen, powerful, evil personalities. Feelings of guilt, fear, self-loathing, and restlessness often are identified by the tormented. We can imagine that Mary was depressed and lost her will to live. There may have been a constant struggle between what she knew was right and the things she was driven to do. Did she have a penchant for antisocial behavior? Undoubtedly, she was embarrassed and ashamed. She liked nothing about herself; she felt cursed and confused.

After Jesus delivered her, we can picture her as being overwhelmed with two realizations. First, she was clean: the inner emotional turbulence had ended, and her tormented soul was at peace. Second, she was given the gift of dignity and value. After years of hopelessness, she found someone who could free her. Someone who saw in her something worth saving, redeeming, and loving. It was Someone whose opinion counted much more than that of all of her peers combined.

Mary's transformation was remarkable. She probably even looked younger; the weight of the world had been lifted from her fragile shoulders. It no longer mattered what others thought of her. She had met a man who had the power to change her life. Now she would devote herself to following and serving Him.

A FOLLOWER OF JESUS

As far as we know, Mary never returned to Magdala again. If she did, it was only for a brief visit. She became part of an inner circle of women, including Joanna, the wife of Herod's steward, and Susanna. Some names were listed in Luke, others were not.

We must remember this when we feel insignificant and when our names are not recorded or honored. Not all faithful people had their names recorded in the Bible, even if they lived during the time of Jesus. Our names might never be in a newspaper or on a speaking roster, but God knows who we are, and we are just as special to Him as Mary was.

We read, "These women were helping to support them out of their own means" (Luke 8:3). They not only ministered to Jesus and His disciples financially, but personally and spiritually as well. The word *helping*, sometimes translated *minister*, is actually *diaokinos* in Greek, from which we get the word *deaconess*. Paul calls Phoebe a *diaokinos* in Romans 16:1. These women who helped Jesus were the original deaconesses.

Jesus and His colleagues needed money in order to live; after all, they didn't receive wages for traveling and sharing the Good News. Jesus Himself was not reimbursed for His speeches and miracles. These women supported Him by offering prayers, obtaining and preparing food, and showing their helpfulness through acts of kindness and encouragement. From town to town, village to village, often living in the open fields or caves, these women went along to help. Mary was a member of Jesus' entourage, this group of women who traveled with Him and provided for Him.

The rabbis would never have condoned this. Women were viewed as untrustworthy and seductive; in fact, they were usually blamed for men's lusts and any adulterous relationships that might ensue. So it's probable that the official religious leadership thought it improper to travel with what could be misinterpreted as a harem. But Jesus would not allow men to blame women for their sexual indiscretions and lusts. When He said, "But I tell you that anyone who looks at a woman lustfully has already committed adultery with her in his heart" (Matthew 5:28), Jesus was putting the blame for men's unholy desires squarely upon their own shoulders. *They* had the responsibility of controlling themselves and, if necessary, gouging out their eyes to keep from sinning (v. 29).

In a blatant countercultural move, Jesus made sure that women were not treated as outcasts or unworthy of ministry. Traveling in a group insured that the entourage maintained proper decorum. And we can be sure that the very presence of Jesus would prevent any impropriety. But He would not shield Himself or His disciples from the presence of women who had a godly zeal to help in ministry.

But second—and this is important—the other rabbis would

not have traveled with such an entourage because women were viewed as "weak-minded." One sect of the Pharisees would pray every morning, "God, I thank you that I am not a woman." What is more, a man only had to clap his hands three times to legally divorce his wife for something as trivial as burning the bread. The prevailing attitude was that women were deemed worthy only to bear children and serve the male species.

Jesus thought differently.

The oft-misinterpreted biblical teaching of male headship has frequently caused men to look upon women with feelings of superiority. Whether by the Pharisees during the time of Jesus or the present leadership in some churches, women have often felt restricted in exercising their gifts. However, many have overcome such discouragements and have achieved great things in the name of Christ. Like Mary Magdalene, they have risen above their limitations to play an important role in the spread of the gospel.

Consider these examples: a woman named Fabiola founded the first Christian hospital in Europe; Amy Carmichael opened a Christian orphanage for abused girls in India; and a newly widowed Elisabeth Elliot lived with the remote Ecuadorean tribe who had murdered her husband, in order to translate the New Testament into their language.

We know that Jesus would applaud these gifted women, and many more throughout church history. Their vision and determination motivated them to do great things for the sake of the Kingdom.

AT THE CROSS

From the beginning of their association with Jesus, these women evidently continued helping Him right up to the Crucifixion.

Speaking of that event, we read, "Many women were there, watching from a distance. They had followed Jesus from Galilee to care for his needs. Among them were Mary Magdalene, Mary the mother of James and Joses, and the mother of Zebedee's sons" (Matthew 27:55-56). It is noteworthy that Mary Magdalene is not singled out in any way as having greater importance or being more special to Jesus. At great personal risk, all of these women came as close as they dared to the gruesome crucifixion of their friend and Savior.

The depth of Mary Magdalene's commitment can be gauged by her presence at the cross. John the apostle describes the scene: "Near the cross of Jesus stood his mother, his mother's sister, Mary the wife of Clopas, and Mary Magdalene" (John 19:25). Together they stand, weeping and watching in horror. This was not a place for a woman to be; for that matter, it was not a place for a man to be.

Mel Gibson's movie *The Passion of the Christ* has changed the way we view the suffering of those who were crucified. It was probably difficult for the women to get near Jesus' cross because of the band of soldiers and the crush of the mob. But as time passed, the crowd thinned and the women stepped as close as they could, "until they finally stood where they could hear the low moans of His suffering, see the blood slowly dripping from His wounds, and there they hear the low exhausted tones in which He committed His mother Mary to His apostle John."[1]

Evidently, when Christ released His mother to John, most of the women left shortly thereafter. But two women refused to leave. One was the mother of James and Joses, and the other was Mary Magdalene. They stayed until after Jesus died and His body was taken away.

Joseph of Arimathea, a secret follower of Jesus, asked the Roman governor Pilate for the body of Jesus. Pilate granted him his request. With the help of a man named Nicodemus, another follower of Jesus, Joseph took down the body from the cross. The two men prepared Jesus' body with expensive spices, wrapped it in linen cloth, and placed it in Joseph's own garden tomb, newly cut out of rock. "Then he rolled a stone against the entrance of the tomb. Mary Magdalene and Mary the mother of Joses saw where he was laid" (Mark 15:46-47).

Last to leave the cross; first to see Him laid in the tomb.

Mary loved this man, Jesus, who gave her a new beginning— a man who forgave her past and offered her an eternal future. He also restored her dignity by allowing her to help Him in His ministry. The intensity of her love was a direct result of the deliverance and forgiveness she had received. Forgiven much, she loved much.

Mary, like the twelve disciples, was unprepared for Christ's death. When Jesus predicted He was about to die, His core group of followers simply refused to believe His words, insisting that it could not be true. They found it difficult, if not impossible, to believe that the Messiah could be so helpless as to be overcome by evil men. During their time with Jesus, they had concluded that He could always outwit His enemies. They had seen it with their own eyes. But now Jesus was dead. They were devastated. And if they did not expect His death, they most assuredly did not expect a resurrection.

Mary waited until the end of the Jewish Sabbath before she and the other women crept through the predawn darkness to the tomb were the body of Jesus had been laid. Customarily, women would prepare a body for burial by placing spices next to it. So Mary came looking for the body of Jesus to complete that task. How grateful we are that she did not find what she was looking for!

Mary also came to the tomb to find answers to her questions. How could the One who had the power to deliver her from seven demons be dead? How could the man she trusted no longer be there for her? How could the Messiah die a horrible, unjust death? "When they hounded Jesus and hung Him on a cross, they really showed how helpless God is. When the chips are down, Mary told herself, a person is alone and deserted."[2]

THE RESURRECTION

When Mary arrived at the tomb, she did not think that anything unusual had happened. Grief distorts reality. Mary was not looking for the living Christ, she was looking for a dead one.

Suddenly a man addressed her. Thinking he was a gardener, she asked, "Sir, if you have carried him away, tell me where you have put him, and I will get him" (John 20:15).

"Mary." The man called her by name.

Christ, the Good Shepherd, "calls his own sheep by name and . . . they know his voice" (John 10:3-4). Jesus' relationship with us is always personal. We are born into an impersonal world, given a number on our cribs, then later another number on our death certificate. In between those two events, our identities are defined by numbers such as a social security number and credit card numbers. If we are not careful, someone might steal our identities. But Jesus knows who we are, personally and confidentially. He calls us by our first name, just as He did with Mary.

Mary quickly turned and "cried out in Aramaic, '*Rabboni!*' (which means Teacher)" (John 20:16, emphasis added).

Jesus said, "Do not hold on to me, for I have not yet returned to the Father" (v. 17). She was shocked to see Him and reached out to touch Him, possibly grasping His feet. Jesus told her to stop touching Him, for He had not yet gone up into the presence of His Father. The nature of their relationship had changed. He was no longer the earthly Jesus, but a heavenly Jesus in transition.

This is the only time in the New Testament that Jesus and Mary Magdalene were alone together. Standing in His presence she was blessed in two ways:

First, Jesus called Mary His sister when He said, "Go instead to my brothers and tell them, 'I am returning to my Father and your Father, to my God and your God'" (v. 17). Obviously, since God is *His* father and God is *her* father, that makes Mary His sister. This is also the first time He called His disciples *brothers*, giving explicit expression to the new family that had been created. Jesus is the "elder brother" and we are all a part of the family.

Second, Jesus gave Mary an assignment, "*Go* to my brothers." *She* is to return to tell the disciples what she has seen and heard. This woman is the first witness to the Resurrection, the first one to carry the news to others. *The doctrine that is at the heart of Christianity was first proclaimed by a woman!*

Why did Jesus choose Mary to deliver this joyful message? Most likely, there are several reasons. Primarily, He chose her because of her faithfulness. She did not deny Him as Peter did. She did not forsake Him as the disciples had. She stayed near the cross as He was dying. She went to the tomb to anoint His body. She was willing to search for His missing body.

Jesus also chose Mary because of her love for Him. She loved Jesus, not in a romantic way, but with a love stemming from gratefulness and devotion for what He had done for her. He had freed her from a prison of demonic affliction and torment. He had dramatically and completely changed her life and given her something to live for. No wonder she loved Him so deeply! Wouldn't you? Those of us who have been set free and forgiven of our sins love Him deeply, as well. *Every sinner has a past; every saint has a future.*

And then, not to be overlooked, the fact was that she was the only one at the tomb at that very moment. Mary had gained the right to be honored as one of the greatest women of New Testament history. This, by the way, is one proof of the narrative's historicity. No Jewish author in the ancient world would have invented a story with a woman as the first witness to the most important event in Christendom! In fact, the Jews did not accept the testimony of a woman; it was deemed invalid in and out of court. No wonder Mary recruited other women to go with her to tell the disciples the news.

Quite predictably, the disciples did not believe Mary and the other women when they said Jesus was alive. "But they did not believe the women, because their words seemed to them like nonsense" (Luke 24:11). Jesus was, in effect, saying to Mary, "They don't trust you, but I do. . . . . I know that you are a woman of integrity; I know that you are worthy of bearing a message for Me."

All four Gospels insist that Jesus first appeared to women. Darrell Bock writes, "This detail, running against the larger, ancient culture as it does, is one of the key evidences that these resurrection stories were not invented by a church trying to give Jesus a higher status than he really had."[3] Jesus shattered the stereotypes.

Leonard Swindler says that in choosing Mary to proclaim the Resurrection, Jesus is clearly rejecting the second-class status of women. The effort of Jesus to connect women with His gospel, he writes, "is so obvious that it is an overwhelming tribute to man's intellectual myopia not to have discerned it effectively in two thousand years."[4] This event was a great affirmation of women's value and merit.

Mary was changed by the Resurrection. We've all met people who have had to stand beside the grave of a little child or another loved one and wonder how they could carry on. The Resurrection assures us that someday these graves will be as empty as His own. "Because I live, you also will live" (John

14:19). To stand at the Cross and not know that there is a Resurrection would be cause for despair. But like Mary, who proclaimed, "I have seen the Lord!" we can be certain that the Christ we love is alive and that we will spend eternity with Him.

Jesus was drawn to those who were powerless, those who were marginalized, those who needed help and admitted it. The same is true today. In ancient times, women were also drawn to Jesus. "His purity of soul, His reverent courtesy to the [opposite] sex, His championship of their equal dignity with men before God, and His demand for supreme zeal in all in the spread of the New Kingdom, drew them after Him."[5]

Hebrews 13:8 says, "Jesus Christ is the same yesterday and today and forever." Jesus is the same man today for all the same reasons. We can trust Him, just as the women of Jesus' day found Him to be a man they could trust.

And subsequently He found them to be trusted friends. Jesus broke with precedent and gave them an expanding role in the church. He let them help Him, and they demonstrated devotion and dependability. When the mother of James and John came to Him with a question, He listened politely. Every woman who encountered Jesus felt validated and worthy because He gave them His full attention. Today He asks women to come out of the shadows and serve Him to the best of their abilities, utilizing their gifts. Mary Magdalene is proof that *who we are does not determine who we shall be.*

She also reminds us that Jesus can be near without our knowing it. We walk in the midst of the ascended Christ. He is at our side. He calls our name, but we might be too busy to hear it. Through circumstances, through suffering, through a friend, and especially through the New Testament narratives, He speaks and wants us to hear. He is nearer to us than we know.

We can agree that women have made significant contributions throughout church history. One that has been overlooked is hymn writing. In some cases, these hymns are sung in churches where women are not allowed to speak. One such hymn writer is Jennie Evelyn Hussey, who lived in New Hampshire during the early 1900s. She spent most of her life caring for her invalid sister even though she herself suffered from crippling arthritis. When the pain was almost too much to bear, she wrote a memorable poem called "Lead Me to Calvary" that would give her a place among the great poets of our time. We sing:

> May I be willing Lord to bear
> Daily my cross for thee.
> Even thy cup of grief to share
> Lead me to Calvary.

But the stanza that we can use as our own prayer is this one:

> Let me like Mary through the gloom
> Come with a gift for thee.
> Show to me now the empty tomb
> Lead me to Calvary.

Mary teaches us that we have to move beyond the Cross to the empty tomb. There, through our tears, we encounter hope and help as Jesus calls our names. And when we hear our names, we are invited to share the Good News of Jesus with everyone who crosses our path.

A PRAYER

Yes, Father, like Mary, I want to peer into the empty tomb of Jesus and experience the assurance that you are standing beside me despite my own disappointments and loneliness. I thank you that you lifted Mary out of a private dungeon to give her hope and healing. That is my prayer for myself and all those around me who also stand in need of a touch of your grace. I thank you for your love and companionship. In Jesus' name, Amen.

Now [Jesus] had to go through Samaria. So he came to a town in Samaria called Sychar, near the plot of ground Jacob had given to his son Joseph. Jacob's well was there, and Jesus, tired as he was from the journey, sat down by the well. It was about the sixth hour.

When a Samaritan woman came to draw water, Jesus said to her, "Will you give me a drink?" (His disciples had gone into the town to buy food.)

The Samaritan woman said to him, "You are a Jew and I am a Samaritan woman. How can you ask me for a drink?" (For Jews do not associate with Samaritans.)

Jesus answered her, "If you knew the gift of God and who it is that asks you for a drink, you would have asked him and he would have given you living water."

"Sir," the woman said, "you have nothing to draw with and the well is deep. Where can you get this living water? Are you greater than our father Jacob, who gave us the well and drank from it himself, as did also his sons and his flocks and herds?"

Jesus answered, "Everyone who drinks this water will be thirsty again, but whoever drinks the water I give him will never thirst. Indeed, the water I give him will become in him a spring of water welling up to eternal life."

The woman said to him, "Sir, give me this water so that I won't get thirsty and have to keep coming here to draw water."

He told her, "Go, call your husband and come back."

"I have no husband," she replied.

Jesus said to her, "You are right when you say you have no husband. The fact is, you have had five husbands, and the man you now have is not your husband. What you have just said is quite true."

"Sir," the woman said, "I can see that you are a prophet. Our fathers worshiped on this mountain, but you Jews claim that the place where we must worship is in Jerusalem."

Jesus declared, "Believe me, woman, a time is coming when you will worship the Father neither on this mountain nor in Jerusalem. You Samaritans worship what you do not know; we worship what we do know, for salvation is from the Jews. Yet a time is coming and has now come when the true worshipers will worship the Father in spirit and truth, for they are the kind of worshipers the Father seeks. God is spirit, and his worshipers must worship in spirit and in truth."

The woman said, "I know that Messiah" (called Christ) "is coming. When he comes, he will explain everything to us."

Then Jesus declared, "I who speak to you am he."

JOHN 4:4-26

2

JESUS, LOVER OF A DIVORCED WOMAN

Divorce comes even to those who marry with the best of intentions.

Many years ago God placed a dear woman named Ellen in our lives. Throughout her life she has suffered many painful, sorrowful disappointments. Ellen grew up in an abusive, shame-based home with poverty and harsh discipline. She thought she had married well, but her husband's taunts soon turned into cruel and sexually suggestive ridicule, and for more than three years she endured his verbal abuse. One night he accused her of infidelity, severely beat her, and left, taking their daughter with him.

Weeks later, he coerced Ellen into signing divorce papers by threatening her life and the child's. Frightened over what he might do, she signed, not realizing that in doing so, she was giving him custody of their little girl. Unbeknownst to Ellen, her ex-husband kept her from knowing that their daughter was living with his parents only five miles away. I (Rebecca) was with Ellen the day she discovered her ex-husband was taking their daughter away to live in another state. In shock and disbelief, Ellen collapsed on the ground, screaming and mourning the loss of her precious daughter. I turned to Scripture for comfort and hope, but God seemed far away, and Ellen would not be comforted.

Brokenhearted and grieving, Ellen became involved with a man whose wife had left him. He professed to be a Christian, and as soon as his divorce was final, they married. This marriage lasted almost fifteen years, during which time her new husband was unfaithful numerous times. Ellen worked hard each time to forgive him and tried desperately to keep the marriage together for the sake of their two children. But to her sorrow, he finally abandoned them to live with a mean, vindictive woman. Another divorce followed, during which time Ellen went through indescribable humiliation and suffering.

Unemployed, on the verge of homelessness, and suffering severe emotional trauma, Ellen moved several times trying to settle in the best possible place for the sake of the two children she had with her second husband. She worked hard to provide for the family, get the kids through high school, and see that they went to college. It seemed that God was helping and blessing her.

Innocently, a friendship began with a man with whom she worked. He, too, was a wounded person who had experienced trauma, but he had no use for God. Being a fellow survivor, Ellen had great compassion for him and even helped him work through some terrifying memories in his past. They became great friends and helped each other with the everyday challenges of life. She earnestly prayed that he would see his need for God and a Savior.

Eventually, they became romantically involved and talked of marriage. But as the months turned into years, their relationship started to change. He became involved with a cadre of dishonest people and began to see other women. Ellen desperately hoped that he would turn to God, but his behavior was demoralizing to her. Their relationship became characterized by verbal, emotional, and physical abuse. A relationship that had at one time seemed so promising deteriorated into a hideous nightmare.

Once again, Ellen began to walk down the long and painful road of detachment, humiliation, loneliness, and starting over. Once more, God and man had failed her—father, husbands, friends, family. She felt used and abandoned. In pain and desperation, she wanted to die.

But Ellen is alive today, giving thanks to God that even during those years of wandering, searching, and suffering, He did not abandon her. Two divorces, sinful relationships, and children who had been wounded by broken homes—even these did not separate her from God's love.

Just as the woman at the well discovered, Jesus comes to those who are scarred by a sinful past and gives them hope for a better future. He is the lover of the wounded and hopeless, those who live with regret and deep loss.

☉☉

Five failed marriages!

The woman at the well was disillusioned with life in general and with men in particular. She had tried desperately to find the right man, but her choices were limited. She had hoped that each new marriage would be better than the last. But this time it seemed ridiculous to get married again. Men could divorce their wives for frivolous reasons. She couldn't go through that again. It's possible that the man she lived with had a track record no better than her own. Perhaps one or more of her husbands had died, and she had children for whom she needed to provide.

Whatever the details, she was filled with shame, guilt, anger, cynicism—these emotions were her constant companions. She was a failure, a disappointment to her friends and especially to herself. It was bad enough to have such a reputation. But she was also a Samaritan, a despised minority race.

She was heartbroken and lonely, a woman without respect and without rights. Who was she? We know her simply as the Samaritan woman, the woman at the well who woke one morning not knowing that she had a divine appointment.

Undoubtedly, she was the scourge of her town, the woman whom people whispered about in the marketplace. She was born into a tribe of half-breeds, a people in whose veins ran the contaminated blood of the pagan Assyrians. The Jews regarded these Samaritans with contempt; they were worse than the Gentiles, whom they referred to as dogs. Neither this woman's heritage nor her track record had anything to commend her. And yet, Jesus chose her as the first person to whom He would reveal His identity as the Messiah.

JESUS' ITINERARY

In Jesus' day, Palestine was divided into three well-defined areas: Galilee, Judea, and Samaria. When Jesus left Judea to return to Galilee, we read, "Now he had to go through Samaria. So he came to a town in Samaria called Sychar, near the plot of ground Jacob had given to his son Joseph. Jacob's well was there, and Jesus, tired as he was from the journey, sat down by the well. It was about the sixth hour" (John 4:4–6).

Between Judea in the south and Jesus' destination of Galilee in the north, was the territory of Samaria, a sore spot in the life of the Jewish nation. Racial hatred dated back to 722 BC when the Assyrians had come and carried thousands of Jews back with them into their own land before repopulating this area of Israel with their own pagan people. Inevitably, there was intermarriage, and their progeny were regarded as a disgrace to the purity of the Jewish stock.

The Jews actually refused to walk through Samaria. They would cross the Jordan River at its southern tip near the Dead Sea, then make their way up the east side of the river through the territory that was later called "Trans-Jordan." Then they would cross the river again farther north near Galilee, avoiding Samaria altogether. Why? Because Samaria was out of their comfort zone due to prejudice and paganism. Any self-respecting Jew wanted to be sure that he did not walk on contaminated soil. Even Samaritan bread was referred to as swine's flesh.

There was also a religious barrier. The Samaritans were not welcome in Jerusalem to worship at the Temple. Being a despised minority, they didn't travel to Jerusalem for the feast days. So they set up their own rival religion, complete with an altar on Mt. Gerizim, located about a half mile from Jacob's well. Over time, their religion degenerated into paganism.

Today, unfortunately, avoiding anyone who practices a different religion or whose lifestyle clashes with our cherished convictions is often the norm. Rather than entering their world with the gospel, we are tempted to keep to ourselves and point our fingers with the same attitude the Jews displayed.

Judea. Galilee. Jerusalem. For the Jews, Samaria was not "on the way" to any of these frequented places. In taking this route, Jesus chose to cross racial, cultural, and religious boundaries to bring hope and deliverance to this woman. That's why we are struck with John's statement about Jesus, "Now he *had* to go through Samaria" (John 4:4). The Greek text is even more emphatic; it contains the little word *dei*, which means "of necessity." Not geographical necessity, but spiritual necessity. It is the same word Jesus used at the age of twelve when He told the doctors of law in Jerusalem, "I *must* be about My Father's business" (Luke 2:49, NKJV, emphasis added).

THE UNEXPECTED REQUEST

Jesus and the disciples were weary, hungry, and thirsty from their journey under the hot Judean sun. Jesus sat down near Jacob's well, while the disciples left to buy food in the nearby town. He was alone as a woman approached with her water jug. "When a Samaritan woman came to draw water, Jesus said to her, 'Will you give me a drink?'" (John 4:7).

This simple request for a drink was a doorway that opened into an extended discussion about her background, her failures, and the gift of living water that was available to all who wanted it. Later, when the disciples returned, they were amazed that Jesus talked alone, in broad daylight, with a woman.

Why the surprise?

Let's take a look at the late second-century AD text called the *Mishna*, a written collection of Jewish oral law that reflects the attitude of the Jews toward women in Jesus' day. The *Mishna* discusses, among other things, how a man should relate to a woman. "Whoever has business with women should not be alone with women" we read. Later it warns, "Don't talk too much to women." The rationale is that such chatter brings trouble to one's self.[1] Rabbis did not even speak to their own wives or daughters in public.

Jesus did not follow these traditions. If we hurry through this story too quickly we just might miss the full significance of what He did in speaking to this Samaritan woman. In this one act, Jesus shattered stereotypes and taboos that had been carefully nurtured for centuries. He gave His attention and time to a woman who would have been ignored by any man, religious or otherwise. He spoke to her—in public—about the secrets of her heart. Jesus had to go where others refused to be seen and do what others could not do.

Who was she? A woman of the despised Samaritan race—immoral, poor, and pagan.

Her emotional burden was heavier than the pitcher of water she planned to carry back into town. Jesus knew that He was the only one who could help her. It was important that He be there when she arrived.

THE PERSONAL DISCUSSION

John tells us that the woman arrived at the well at "the sixth hour." In ancient times, the first hour was six o'clock in the morning. So we can assume that she arrived at the well at noon, when the sun was at its height.

Why is this detail important? The women of the town often fetched water together as a group. Usually, they arrived in the morning to avoid the blistering noon sun. Their custom was to come to the well early and enjoy this social event, a time when they could talk with the other women of the community. They had so few opportunities for socializing that they took advantage of this daily ritual.

So quite possibly this woman arrived alone at the well at midday in order to avoid contact with the other women who had already drawn their water for the day. It is likely that she had been the object of their gossip on other occasions. And although she longed for their friendship, the pain of rejection and scorn kept her away until they had gone.

If only the other women would give her a chance to talk, she could have explained how some of her husbands had divorced her for frivolous reasons, how her desperation to provide for her children had forced her into yet another marriage, how she had been fooled by the promises and lies of men. Actually, she didn't blame the other women for avoiding her. She knew she had a bad reputation around town. Whether it was just or unjust, she was despised and lonely.

Here was a woman who needed to hear what Jesus had to say and to learn what only He could teach her. She needed an invitation to try a new kind of water from a different source, water that would give her a new quality of life. And this unlikely woman would be the means by which many others would find eternal life.

When Jesus asked the Samaritan woman for a drink, she knew immediately that the tired stranger was a Jew. Startled, she said, "You are a Jew and I am a Samaritan woman. How can you ask me for a drink?" (John 4:9). She was not only shocked that a Jew would ask a woman—a Samaritan woman—for a drink, but that Jesus did not have His own cup with Him.

Most travelers of Jesus' day carried a bucket so that they could drink from whatever source of water they found. Jesus probably had one, but the disciples may have taken it to town to get it filled. Another Jewish law forbade Jews from drinking from a vessel that belonged to an outcast because it would make them ceremonially unclean and, in reality, probably physically unclean too.

Jesus avoided a direct reply to her question and said simply, "If you knew the gift of God and who it is that asks you for a drink, you would have asked him and he would have given you living water" (v. 10). There was something about the way He talked and the kindness He showed that attracted her attention. She suspected that He was not just an ordinary man; something was unusual about Him.

Jesus humbled Himself by becoming dependent on this woman. Yes, He was the Son of God, and for that matter He could have created water for Himself. But He wants us to know that *God* is asking a Samaritan woman for a drink.

Quickly, Jesus gained the woman's respect. She now addressed him as *Sir.* But she was still thinking in purely human terms when she asked in verse 11, "Sir, you have nothing to draw with and the well is deep. Where can you get this living water?" (To the Jews, living water meant running water, always preferred over well water, which could be stagnant.)

She continued, "Are you greater than our father Jacob, who gave us the well and drank from it himself, as did also his sons and his flocks and herds?" (v. 12). Any respectable Jew would undoubtedly deny this claim that her people were descendants from Jacob. Jesus, of course, did not become entangled with such questions. He knew she was really asking two questions: How are you going to get this special "living water"? And who are you, *really*?

This is the story of our lives: When God makes a promise to us, we question it, and ask in effect: "'Lord, where is your bucket? . . . how are you going to do it? I don't see that you are prepared to make good on your promise.' Like the Samaritan woman, we really don't know Who we're talking to. We don't understand His power and what He intends to do."[2]

Not all of the promises Jesus makes will be fulfilled during our lifetime. Sometimes we falsely think He has promised us certain things. For instance, He does not promise we'll be wealthy or have physical healing or have everything we want. But He does promise that He loves us dearly; He will always be with us no matter what we are going through; He will provide for our needs in His time and way; He will always forgive us when we confess our sin. Other promises will be fulfilled in the future, but the gift of eternal life that Jesus offered this woman began the moment she accepted it.

If *you* have never received this gift, you can today, right now. Ask Jesus to forgive your sins and be your Savior. This same living water will be yours!

Faith trusts even without a rope and a bucket, and without a sign or an explanation.[3] Jesus does not say, "Lady, you're talking to

Jesus of Nazareth . . . let Me tell you about all the miracles I've performed." He just gives more specifics to His promise. "Everyone who drinks this water will be thirsty again, but whoever drinks the water I give him will never thirst. Indeed, the water I give him will become in him a spring of water welling up to eternal life" (v. 13). She had no idea that she was actually speaking to the Creator of the water!

The Samaritan woman was understandably interested. She would love to receive this water so that she would not have to make the half-mile trek with her water pot every day. No more trips in the heat of the day to draw water alone. If Jesus could give her a kind of water that would constantly slake her thirst, life would indeed be easier. Her body was weary from this chore, and her soul was weary from the shame. Yes, it sounded like a great offer. She had found a man with kindness in His eyes rather than critical superiority.[4]

When Jesus promised she would never thirst again, she wondered what kind of a labor-saving device He might have. In her mind, she saw Jesus as simply a means to get water, just as we are often tempted to use Him for our own ends and purposes.

Jesus still had not told her who He was. She had to be confronted with her need before she could realize that He could help her. If she didn't have a problem, it didn't matter who she was talking to. If you are not sick, you don't care whether you're in the presence of a doctor. At this point it was more important that she understand who *she* really was than who *Jesus* really was.

Jesus exposed her need by a reference to her private life. "Go, call your husband and come back" (v. 16). Jesus knew this woman was hiding sin that needed to be faced. He asked her to bring her husband because He wanted to uncover her pitiful condition. With that request, her private life passed before her as she suddenly recognized her need. She was staggered by Jesus' knowledge of her personal life.

Too wary to tell Him everything, she cautiously admitted, "I have no husband." The words just slipped from her mouth. "You are right when you say you have no husband" (v. 17).

It was true; she didn't have a husband. But sometimes partial truth won't do; the whole truth must be told. You don't simply tell a doctor that you have a cold if you also have malaria. Jesus needed her to admit to the whole sordid story.

"The fact is, you have had five husbands, and the man you now have is not your husband. What you have just said is quite true" (v. 18).

The woman did not cringe; she realized now that He knew all about her—all the wretched details. Nervously, she stated, "Sir, I can see that you are a prophet" (v. 19). She was in effect admitting the truth of what He said. Though she had told Him nothing about herself, Jesus revealed the brokenness of her life. And yet He did not condemn her.

In every one of His personal encounters with women, Jesus knows everything about them, but never condemns them. If He were to condemn those who had failed, either because of their own choices or at the hands of others, He would only be sending them back to their own torture chamber of guilt and anger. Jesus always leads women out of their shame into the light of forgiveness and acceptance.

THE OFFER OF TWO BLESSINGS

The Samaritan woman was invited to participate in two extraordinary blessings. First, she was given living water, which of course has a double meaning. On its most basic level it refers to drinking water that quenches our physical thirst. But this water is also symbolic of God, the wellspring that quenches our spiritual thirst. The Old Testament uses the word *thirst* in referring to the soul's desire for God, and *living water* is a descriptive phrase used for God Himself.

The promise in the Old Testament was that when the Messiah came, people would draw water from the wells of salvation (Isaiah 12:3), and all who were thirsty could come to drink this water (Isaiah 55:1). In every person there is an unsatisfied longing, a vague discontent and emptiness. Augustine said it best, "[O God] you have made us for yourself and our hearts are restless until they find their rest in you."[5]

Jesus was using thirst to show the woman at the well her spiritual need. More than that, He was telling her that the water He could give her was miraculous and would provide her both eternal life and spiritual cleansing. In promising this woman that He could banish her thirst forever, Jesus was making a Messianic claim, "They shall not hunger nor thirst" (Isaiah 49:10, KJV). *This gift of eternal life could be hers for the taking.*

In fact, a few chapters later, at the Feast of Tabernacles, Jesus emphatically gave the same invitation to everyone when He made this awesome claim, "If anyone thirsts, let him come to Me and drink. He who believes in Me, as the Scripture has said, out of his heart will flow rivers of living water" (John 7:37-38, NKJV). *Inner resources for the journey that leads to eternity.*

Unless she had been widowed, not one of this woman's five husbands had loved her enough to stay married. Now she was living with a man who didn't want to marry her—or maybe she didn't want to marry him. Either way, it was an unfulfilling arrangement. Emotionally, she was on her own. She carried the shame and sorrow of her failures alone. Over the years she probably had cried a bucket of tears over these broken relationships.

She had a burning thirst in her heart that was as debilitating as physical thirst could ever be. The thought of having inner resources intrigued her. If this stranger would keep His promise, she could have her own emotional and spiritual reservoir—it would mean grace to cope, energy to carry on, and hope beyond the drudgery of her life.

With this kind of strength, she could leave her live-in companion with the assurance that *she would never be alone again.*

The second blessing Jesus offered was the privilege of becoming a special worshipper of the true God. This pagan woman had been brought up to believe that Mount Gerizim and its altar were sacred and Jerusalem was to be despised. She reminded Jesus that she and her people worshipped on this mountain, but the Jews insisted that all proper worship be done in Jerusalem (v. 20).

Jesus replied, "Believe me, woman, a time is coming when you will worship the Father neither on this mountain nor in Jerusalem. You Samaritans worship what you do not know; we worship what we do know, for salvation is from the Jews. Yet a time is coming and has now come when the true worshipers will worship the Father in spirit and truth, for they are the kind of worshipers the Father seeks. God is spirit, and his worshipers must worship in spirit and in truth" (vv. 21-24).

Jesus led the Samaritan woman from belief in shrines, ceremonies, and unknown deities to the realization of the imminent God who can be worshipped anywhere. If she knew the truth and wanted to worship the true God the right way, then He would invite her to worship Him.

Successful people are often too self-absorbed to be worshippers, and those born into other religions are unable to be "true worshippers." So the Father goes looking for worshipers among the ostracized, among those who have blown it and those who have fallen the farthest.

Imagine! God the Father, seeking this Samaritan woman?

Good men and women had shunned this woman, and according to the Old Testament, she probably was a candidate for stoning. What could this man mean when He spoke about a God who was searching for true worshippers, even among those who have made a mess of their lives?

Success, as we generally think of it, was not available to this woman, but intimacy with God was. She could become dear to the heart of the seeking Father. What a precious picture this gives us of what Jesus does today. He searches among those who are failures, those who have been abused, and those who think there is no hope for them.

This woman lived in a despised area of the country and was of mixed race, yet she was one of the most theologically informed women in the New Testament. She knew the reasons for the hostility between Jews and Samaritans; she knew that one must worship at a valid temple; and she knew about the coming of the Messiah. What she was not sure of was whether *this man* was the One. She expressed her uncertainty, "I know that Messiah" (called Christ) "is coming. When he comes, he will explain everything to us" (v. 25). She was politely saying that she wasn't sure who Jesus was, but when the Messiah arrived, she knew *He* would explain all of this business about how and where to worship.

This is when Jesus chose to reveal Himself by saying, "I who speak to you am he" (v. 26). What a dramatic moment!

Incredibly, this Samaritan woman was the first person to whom Jesus revealed His Messiahship in the Gospel of John. The disciples did not come to the conclusion that Jesus was the Messiah until later in His ministry. This woman, whether she realized it or not, belonged to a select few to whom Jesus, the Lord of Glory, revealed His identity. Not only did Jesus not shrink from entering into conversation with her, but He lavished on this one auditor some of His choicest utterances.[6]

We quickly read on to see her reaction, expecting that she has fallen on her knees to worship Him. Whatever her immediate response might have been, however, remains untold, because at that very moment the disciples returned from the city.

Obviously, the disciples were astonished that Jesus was talking to a woman in public. No doubt, they had been influenced by the rabbis' low view of women that said, "Each time that a man prolongs converse with a woman he causes evil to himself and desists from the law and in the end inherits Gehinnom."[7] They were shocked, perhaps even embarrassed, to see Jesus speaking to a woman, but they also may have been impressed by the woman's reverent response to Jesus' revelation. Stunned, the best they could do was ask, "What do you seek?" or "Why are you talking with her?"

They were getting a lesson in the emancipation of womanhood.

THE IMPACT OF ONE CHANGED LIFE

Not to be deterred, the Samaritan woman hurried away, back to the city to tell others about the amazing man she had met. She was so excited that she left behind her water jug, the symbol of the old life, just as the disciples had left their nets to follow Jesus. Of course, this also meant that she planned on coming back to talk with Jesus again.

We read that she told the people, "Come, see a man who told me everything I ever did. Could this be the Christ?" (v. 29). The Greek text says that she spoke to the *men* of the town, although the word used often refers to people in general. In those days a woman of her reputation would likely not be allowed to mingle with other women, so her audience may have been limited to the men of the town.

By saying she had found a man who knew everything about her, she was confessing her own sinfulness. They all knew the things she had done, and by her honesty she gained credibility. If she had said, "Guess what, I just met the Messiah!" they would have laughed and scorned her. But instead, she was cautious and humble.

She also knew that her testimony was suspect, so she didn't want to presume to try to teach others anything. Because she wanted them to decide for themselves, she put her newfound information in the form of a question: "Could this be the Messiah?" Now they, too, were curious, and she returned with a company of townspeople who wanted to see for themselves. We don't know how many people returned with her, but even if she had just found her five former husbands, that would have made quite an entourage to go to the well to see Jesus.[8]

It mattered little to this woman what others now thought of her; she had met a man who knew her whole story and yet found her worthy of living water and a life of delighting the Father with her worship. And if she could receive these gifts, why not share the Good News with others, even at great personal cost?

Jesus has been so taken up with this encounter that when His disciples urged Him to eat what they had just brought, He refused and said, "I have food to eat that you know nothing about" (v. 32). He was so filled with joy about delivering this woman from her life of bondage that He didn't need to eat. The disciples didn't understand: "Has anyone brought him something to eat?"

Jesus continued, "My food . . . is to do the will of him who sent me and to finish his work" (v. 34). His nourishment was to bring living water to the thirsty—Jesus was simply doing the Father's will.

He had just given hope and forgiveness to an unnamed woman. Someday when we meet her in heaven, we'll be able to ask for the details: what were you thinking when you walked that half mile back to Sychar? And what about that man you were living with . . . did you marry him, or did you tell him that your relationship with Jesus was more important than your relationship with him?

When the delegation came from the town to see Jesus, they also believed in Him, but they made it clear to the woman that it was not because of what she said. "We no longer believe just because of what you said; now we have heard for ourselves, and we know that this man really is the Savior of the world" (v. 42). Literally the Greek says, "Now we believe not because of your chatter . . . but because we have seen him for ourselves." The sequel is that the townspeople invited Jesus to come into town. He stayed there two days, and many more believed.

Why would Jesus choose a woman of such a dubious reputation to be the one to whom He would reveal His identity? Why would He use her so mightily in bringing virtually this whole village to faith in Him? Certainly we can say that she had spiritual perception and a willingness to understand; she was also a candidate for pardon and reciprocal love. Those who are forgiven much are often the best evangelists.

But might it also be that Jesus used the woman at the well to break down the bias that men had toward women? To prove that the time had come for the double standard to end? That God delights in using women to share His message? And that His message is for everyone, including those whose lives have been marred by a history of marital failure?

We should note that the text explicitly says, *"Many believed in him because of the woman's testimony"* (v. 39, emphasis added). Even though they would normally not be inclined to listen to a woman's "chatter," God's plan from all of eternity was to use this woman to bring a troupe of despised Samaritans into the Kingdom. Jesus saw women not just as souls worth saving, but also as individuals whose ministry was of great benefit to the Kingdom. The Samaritan woman is a reminder that we don't have to have a perfect record to be used by God in great ways.

Years ago a young teacher in Alabama held the hand of a little girl who was blind and deaf under a stream of water flowing from a pump, and manually spelled out the word *water.* The teacher's name was Anne Sullivan; the hand belonged to Helen Keller. Years later as a surprise for Miss Keller, her classmates presented a fountain to Radcliffe College on their fiftieth class reunion. Before feeling the water, Helen Keller herself read a Braille inscription mounted on the back of the fountain.

> In memory of Anne Sullivan, teacher extraordinary, who beginning with the word, *water,* opened the girl Helen Keller to the world of sight and sound through touch.

Undoubtedly, the Samaritan woman often returned to the well of Sychar where she first met Jesus, and if we could erect a plaque for this event it might read:

> In memory of Jesus, teacher extraordinary, who beginning with the word *water,* opened to the woman of Samaria the whole world of purpose and forgiveness through himself.[9]

A PRAYER

Heavenly Father, I thank You that Jesus came to give me what I do not have, forgiveness and cleansing so that I can have a personal relationship with God. I thank You that You know all about my past, and yet You invite me to worship You. I embrace You, Jesus, as my Savior and Lord. Give me hidden inner resources to cope with the demands of life. Thank You for the assurance that I can enjoy Your presence both here on earth and eternally in heaven. With humility, I receive all that Jesus came to give me, in faith and love. Amen.

Leaving that place, Jesus withdrew to the region of Tyre and Sidon. A Canaanite woman from that vicinity came to him, crying out, "Lord, Son of David, have mercy on me! My daughter is suffering terribly from demon-possession."

Jesus did not answer a word. So his disciples came to him and urged him, "Send her away, for she keeps crying out after us."

He answered, "I was sent only to the lost sheep of Israel."

The woman came and knelt before him, "Lord, help me!" she said.

He replied, "It is not right to take the children's bread and toss it to their dogs."

"Yes, Lord," she said, "but even the dogs eat the crumbs that fall from their masters' table."

Then Jesus answered, "Woman, you have great faith! Your request is granted." And her daughter was healed from that very hour.   MATTHEW 15: 21-28

3

JESUS, LOVER OF A
PERSISTENT MOTHER

Several years ago Louise, a sweet Christian mother, came to us in anguish over her young daughter, seeking comfort and hope. Through her tears she told us that after her second daughter was born, her husband abandoned her and the two children. She was frightened and destitute with no money to pay the mortgage or utilities. She finally moved to another state to live near her sister. Meanwhile, her cruel husband allowed the bank to proceed with the foreclosure of their house, but at the last redeemable moment he made all the delinquent payments and claimed the house. Then, as sole owner, he moved his live-in girlfriend into the house, along with her children. Then he filed for divorce, suing Louise for all court costs.

While the divorce was pending, the court ordered equal visitation rights. This meant that he could pick up the girls—a one-year-old and a thirteen-year-old—at an appointed time and drive them in his truck three hours back to their former house. As her husband drove away, the baby screamed inconsolably, and the frightened teenager pleaded with her mother to intervene. But Louise was helpless to stop him.

Louise's cries and prayers pierced the deafening silence as she begged God to take care of her precious children. She cried out to God for more than an hour, as the sun set and darkness closed in around her. Her courage and faith were tested over and over again, as this scene was repeated many times in the subsequent months. Often, she was on her face before God, begging Him to bring her children back safely. She never lost hope; she never stopped asking God to protect her girls; she never stopped believing that God could change her circumstances.

When the divorce was final, an unwise judge ordered that the ex-husband have lengthy, unsupervised visitation rights. The youngest daughter had to spend several weeks a year with him and his common-law wife. While there, the little girl was neglected by the adults and sexually abused by the woman's children. Louise did everything she could legally to keep her daughter from going into this horrible situation. She reported the facts to the child protection authorities and appealed to the courts for intervention, but the investigation dragged out over many months.

With a broken heart Louise asked me (Rebecca), "How could a loving God allow an innocent child to be abused?" I held her in my arms and wept with this dear woman, her pain and despair were so real. As I prayed for wisdom, a passage from 1 Peter came to mind, and I shared it with Louise: "So then, those who suffer according to God's will should commit themselves to their faithful Creator and continue to do good" (1 Peter 4:19). As we discussed the meaning of these words and prayed together, Louise's countenance relaxed, her fear diminished, and peace came to her heart.

Eventually, the father's visitation rights were rescinded. In retaliation, he stopped sending child support, which Louise desperately needed. But she was fearful that if she took legal action, her ex-husband would attempt to take custody of their youngest child, declaring that she couldn't provide for the children.

Jesus did not relieve Louise's trials, but He has walked with her through them. When everything was against Louise, she fervently believed God was for her. Thankfully, the abused daughter is doing well and is now a lovely teenager who has a heart for God.

If you could meet Louise today, you would find her to be a woman of great faith—the result of great hardships. She does not love Jesus less because of the trials that have come her way; she loves Him more. Like the woman of SyroPhoenicia, Louise's persistence has moved the heart of Jesus, and He has not turned a deaf ear. To this very day, she cries out to God on behalf of her grandchildren who live in difficult circumstances. Even her unanswered prayers have brought comfort and assurance.

∞

There are moments of opportunity that might never come our way again. Time changes circumstances, and we change along with it. Whether it is a marriage proposal, a business venture, or an opportunity to find the answer to our deepest longings, we've all wished we could turn the clock back.

That was certainly true for a desperate mother who lived twenty centuries ago. She took the chance that was offered to her and made the most of it. When we read the story of the Canaanite mother, we marvel at her remarkable persistence and faith, pitted against incredible odds. Her story is carefully documented in the New Testament.

Jesus always treated people with respect, no matter what their spiritual or physical need was. He gently asked questions to reveal what was in their hearts. He was as interested in their motives for seeking Him as He was in their need itself. He loved shattering the barriers of race, gender, and tradition to help women who were in the greatest predicaments.

However, His most puzzling encounter was the one He had with the Canaanite mother who was desperate to get help for her tormented child. Initially, His words sound almost rude and unkind. In fact, this story has sometimes been used in an attempt to prove that Jesus Himself was a sinner just like the rest of us. Some would argue that Jesus had bad days too, and when He did, those around Him felt the sting of His anger and rebuke.

But we believe that *because* this encounter is so unlike Jesus, we have to find within the story itself a better explanation for His response. A superficial reading might lead to the conclusion that Jesus was racist, but thoughtful reflection considers the end of the story, showing that Jesus blessed this woman who won His heart.

Jesus had reasons for His initial reluctance to help her, but in the end He gave her more than she could have asked for. In her attempt to get His attention, this mother was rebuffed. But her faith was not shaken, and ultimately her persistence and faith won His heart.

The geographical setting of this story is remarkable. Jesus had just fed five thousand people with a few loaves and fish near the shores of the Sea of Galilee. That night His disciples were caught in a storm on the lake, and He came to them, walking on the water. Later a delegation from the Pharisees came from Jerusalem, questioning Him about His teaching and motives. He knew that a plot to kill Him was developing.

Then we read, "Leaving that place, Jesus withdrew to the region of Tyre and Sidon" (Matthew 15:21). These cities are located toward the northwest, along the coast of the Mediterranean Sea (today they are still in existence in Lebanon). The walk from the Galilee area would have taken several days over rugged terrain. It was unusual indeed for a delegation of Jewish men to go into territory where the heathen lived.

We are told that Jesus withdrew to this area, probably for a respite and to help the disciples process the news of His impending death. But there was another reason He was walking so far—

He knew there was a woman, far away and in great need, who could not come to Him; He needed to go to her. There is no record of any other contact or activity that Jesus had in this particular area of the country. That He would go so far out of His way shows that this meeting must have been another divine appointment. Jesus made a special trip to bring hope and healing to a specific mother and child.

As further evidence that this woman was the reason for His trip, we read that after the miracle, "Jesus left there and went along the Sea of Galilee" (v. 29). Of course, we don't know how long Jesus and His disciples had stayed, but we are left with the impression that they immediately returned to their customary area of ministry. The Son of God made a time-consuming, strenuous trip for just one woman and her daughter!

Even today, Jesus seeks us out. He does not have to travel to find us geographically, for He fills the universe by His Spirit. He comes to us in our desperate need, our despair, and our tears. He initiates a friendship and becomes our companion along the perilous journey of life. He can arrange a divine appointment with us, just as He did with the woman in this account.

This story is a beautiful illustration of love and compassion. Jesus knew all about this woman and her difficult life. He placed Himself within her reach. She could never have traveled that distance with a sick child to reach Him. In fact, due to racial, religious, and social barriers, it would have been impossible for her to even enter the area where most of Jesus' ministry was taking place.

Somehow, word that Jesus was in the area was already circulating within the community. This mother knew this would be her only chance to test what she had heard about His miracles; she knew she must seek Him out to heal her child. The river of mercy was flowing in her direction, and she took advantage of it.

We are surprised at how much she knew about Jesus and the

spirit world. She called Jesus "The Son of David," which is a messianic title. How could she know this? She lived in a Canaanite culture that was hostile toward the Jews and their Scripture. But rumors of Jesus being the Messiah had reached her ears. With such credentials, she believed that this man was capable of the miracle her daughter needed.

She explained that her daughter was possessed by an evil spirit. We must not write off these references to satanic influence as the vestiges of a superstitious age when modern psychiatry had not yet been discovered. We read in chapter 1 how Jesus exorcized seven spirits from Mary Magdalene.

But why would this Canaanite child have evil spirits? Perhaps there was occultism in the family; perhaps someone had put this child under a curse; or more likely the idolatry of the Canaanites invited evil spirits to torment the worshippers. We can't be sure.

This unnamed woman might have been a single mother trying to find help for her distraught child. She spared no effort to get to Jesus and in doing so she overcame the natural reticence that women had in that culture. In the end, she received the "Great Faith Award" from Jesus.

OVERCOMING THE BARRIERS

In order to appreciate the enormity of the obstacles in this mother's path, let's look at the barriers she had to overcome to approach Jesus.

Men did not recognize women in public; nor were their needs considered important enough for a serious male response.

First, there was the attitude barrier. For reasons unknown to us, this mother approached Jesus alone. Perhaps her husband was dead or no longer connected to the family. On the other hand, she may have reasoned that if she shared her idea with her husband, he would have, at the very least, laughed at her, and at the worst, forbidden her to go. She was doing the best she could in a male-dominated world. To whom else could she go? Perhaps she had already taken her daughter to doctors or to the priests at the temple. If so, they were obviously unable to help her.

If you are a single mother, consider this woman your sister. Her example invites you to seek help from outside your situation. Single mothers sometimes feel isolated and don't know where to turn for help with family problems. The first source of help and comfort is always God, then trusted friends or a pastor, and finally, social and medical services in the community. When your situation seems hopeless, Jesus is a good risk.

There was the race barrier. This mother was a Canaanite, a member of such a corrupt race that centuries earlier God had told the military commander, Joshua, to destroy them. Modern archaeology helps us understand such a sweeping command. The Canaanites had degenerated into incredible cruelty and sexual perversion such as that found only on the outer fringes of our own sexually-obsessed age. But not all of them were killed; many survived in various parts of the land, living as best they could as a despised minority.

There are many Old Testament passages that record how the remaining Canaanites were a source of evil and temptation to the Israelites. In fact, at times the nation of Israel turned from Jehovah and worshipped the Canaanites' god Baal. This was a serious offense to God and He punished the Israelites severely. We can understand, then, why the Jews called them "dogs," a term of derision that is lost in our modern culture where dogs occupy a place of respect. In the Middle East, many dogs were diseased and scrawny scavengers who were hunted and killed. To call someone a dog was to hold that person in utter contempt.

There were no excuses for such prejudice, though there were

reasons. Keep in mind that God had made a covenant with the Jewish people, promising that the Messiah would come through their lineage. Along with this, the blessing that the Jews received was to spill over to the Gentiles, for God said to Abraham, "in you all the nations of the earth will be blessed"(see Genesis 12:3).

The Jews were to take these undeserved blessings and invite the Gentiles to believe in Jehovah. But the Jews thought that God chose them because they were better than others, and as a result, hoarded the blessings for themselves. With few exceptions, they arrogantly saw others as undeserving of God's care. The racial barrier between them and the Gentiles was formidable.

This woman overcame this barrier without an invitation from the Jewish community. She might have said, "I would rather have a sick child then to subject myself to their contempt and hatred." But this mother was not intimated by the racial chasm that separated her from God's hard-hearted but chosen people.

The third barrier was her religion. Baalbak was the citadel of Canaanite worship, not far from Tyre and Sidon. Today, tourists can still see the statue of the god Baal. He is surrounded by temple ruins whose columns pierce the bright blue sky. Religion was the center of Canaanite life. They practiced what could be called sympathetic worship; that is, they believed that they honored their god best by doing what he did. Since Baal was perceived to be a god who practiced immorality of all kinds, worshipping him often degenerated into sexual orgies and debauchery of every type.

This woman and her ancestors had lived in the grip of such pagan worship for centuries. But as powerful as he was thought to be, Baal could not drive out evil spirits. This mother could receive no help from a god of stone. If anything, Baal epitomized worship of evil spirits—a religion not hospitable to other deities. Understandably, the Canaanite woman may have feared retaliation if she sought help outside of her religion. She could have said, "I was born a worshipper of Baal; I will die a worshipper of Baal." But thankfully, she was willing to enlist the help of a Jewish Messiah who represented a different God. This woman had the humility to cross the religious boundary and solicit help from the God of her Jewish enemies. Her example reminds us that sometimes we have to break out of our religious traditions to get to Jesus. We as Christians are often guilty of the same sin—our traditions of "dos and don'ts" can be barriers for those who want to get to Jesus. Sometimes it is difficult for us to separate our own religious subculture from the truth about Jesus.

This woman had to overcome one more barrier: Jesus and His disciples. When Jesus arrived in this town, He took refuge in a house and did not want anyone to know He was there. Perhaps there would have been opposition to His presence, or perhaps a great crowd would have gathered, begging for healing. The fragrance of His life most certainly reached this woman who could not be helped by any other. "Like perfume betrays itself, so He whose name is perfume cannot be hid."[1] When this distraught woman appeared and began pleading for help, we read Jesus "answered her not a word" (v. 23, KJV). He could have healed her child immediately, but first He wanted to test her. Jesus wanted to draw out the courage and faith that lay deep within her heart. In fact, her faith was more important to Him than the healing that was about to take place. Would she give in to fear, religious superstition, or the unkindness of the disciples? Or even His own caustic remarks?

THE SILENCE OF GOD

What are we to do when God is silent? This woman tells us that we must continue worshipping, asking, and believing. Even in our pain, confusion, doubt, and fear, we can come to Him with a humble attitude. God is listening. He is testing us, to see what is in our hearts. He wants us to verbalize our need, and to be willing to do whatever He asks of us, *before* He meets our need. We should never think that the silence of God means that He is indifferent to our need.

The silence of Jesus did not deter this Canaanite mother. She kept crying all the more. By now the disciples picked up on Jesus' nonresponsive attitude. If the Master would not speak with her, then she should be silenced. "Send her away, for she keeps crying out after us" (v. 23). It irritated their sensibilities that an unclean, foreign woman would continue wailing, insisting that their Master take note of her and grant her request. But this mother was determined to get His attention, no matter what.

Jesus then gave a reason for His silence: "I was sent only to the lost sheep of Israel" (v. 24). This, of course, was true; Jesus came to the Jews of His day inviting them to believe His messianic claims. Indeed, when the disciples were sent out in twos they were especially forbidden to go outside of Israel (Matthew 10:5-6). But the intention was that the Jews themselves were to respond to the message of the Kingdom and then be missionaries beyond their borders. Needless to say, the ultimate mission of Jesus was to include the whole world in the offer of His redemption. On many occasions He made it clear that His death and resurrection were for people of all nations and tribes.

At this point we would expect this woman to walk away in deep disappointment. Jesus, whom she perceived to be the Messiah, seemed to be in agreement with the Jews of the day, refusing to bless those who were outside of the chosen nation. But this audacious woman persisted. She came in humility, kneeling before Him and crying but three words, *"Lord, help me!"*

If Jesus was Messiah, He was also Lord. She was more theologically astute than some of His followers! This woman with no temple, no sacrifices, and no Scriptures heard of Jesus and believed what she was told. Her desperation was motivated by her firm conviction that the man before her was well qualified to heal her daughter. She would not let this moment pass, no matter how uncomfortable the conversation became.

Jesus gave her no encouragement, and instead gave this most startling reply: "It is not right to take the children's bread and toss it to their dogs" (v. 26). He knew what she wanted, but rebuked her. He was saying that the Jews were God's children, and the Gentiles were dogs, so what right did she have to ask for a special blessing? Harsh as it seems, we know that Jesus does nothing that is unloving or without a divine purpose.

Perhaps she was encouraged by the fact that Jesus did not use the usual word for *dogs*, which referred to the mangy scavengers of the time. The word He chose could be translated *puppies*, often a reference to household pets. There is no doubt that even when He turned a deaf ear, Jesus was planning to show mercy toward her.

She still did not take offense and walk away, saying, "If that's how You feel about me, I'm out of here." Think of how far she had come: bearing His silence and enduring His dismissal, "I was sent only to the lost sheep of Israel." Now she had to overcome the epithet of being called a *dog*, or at least a puppy. Today, we are easily offended by anyone who disagrees with us, even if it's done politely. Yet this woman was not deterred with what could have been interpreted as an offensive remark. She did not lose sight of her goal. She was not demanding, but persistent, as she humbled herself in the presence of Jesus.

She boldly pressed on by agreeing with Him, then humbly said, "Yes, Lord . . . but even the dogs eat the crumbs that fall from their masters' table" (v. 27). She defended her request by arguing that though she could not be at the same table as the Jews, she at least was worthy of being a puppy under the table. She did not question why it was so; she showed no evidence of resentment because life isn't fair.

She was saying, in effect, "I am not asking for a meal, I am just asking for a few crumbs." She did not want what the children would *eat*, only what they would *discard*. She did not want her gain to be their loss; by all means the children must be well fed. She would be satisfied with the crumbs that fell from the table— a tiny leftover of Jesus' great power.

Jesus could no longer contain himself. " 'Woman, you have great faith! Your request is granted.' And her daughter was healed from that very hour" (v. 28).

Martin Luther said, "She used the master's words against him and won his heart." Someone else has said that her faith scaled the walls of heaven and touched the heart of deity. She got more than the crumbs she asked for. In her persistence she got the whole loaf. "The Lord of Glory surrendered to the faith of a woman."[2]

THE FLOWER OF FAITH

Although this flower of faith was planted in the desert, it grew to become a sweet fragrance to God. This woman shows that true faith is not limited to those who stand in the stream of blessing. Those who persist receive from God what they believe He has promised. Only two people in the Gospel of Matthew are commended by Jesus for having *great* faith. Both were Gentiles: the centurion in Matthew 8:10 and the woman in this story.

At what point would you or I have given up, backed away to weep for ourselves, or sought help from some other source with false hope?

There is a great lesson in perseverance here. We must keep

on coming to Jesus to find the answers for the dilemmas of our lives. We must believe that He has the power to change a hardened heart, to heal a broken relationship, to restore lost purity, to bring hope to a hopeless situation. Jesus' love for women has not changed. He seeks those who are desperate, those who have no one else to go to. We must choose not to be discouraged by His silence, by our unworthiness and guilt, or by the misunderstandings of others.

Perhaps this was also intended to be a lesson for the disciples. Jesus once again included a despised woman in His ministry. And what seemed to be an exercise in prejudice turned out to be an example of how Gentiles are to be included in His family of faith. The disciples hoped that He would heal the Jewish masses and spend most of His time with them. These out-of-the-way, private encounters with hurting, needy women made them nervous.

But that's how Jesus is. He will go anywhere to find those who are desperate. He goes to unlikely places to find those women who may not be able to come to Him due to social, sinful, religious, or racial barriers. Everyone who comes to Him with an empty heart can leave filled. While others come to Jesus with a closed legalistic attitude, "she comes empty-handed and without merit, but open to Jesus. And she is rewarded as He shatters the wall between Jew and Gentile in granting her request for her daughter."[3]

Where does Jesus go today? Through the vision and leadership of a woman in our church, a ministry called Kid's Club was begun in the heart of one of Chicago's most notorious neighborhoods. Thanks to a dedicated staff and hundreds of volunteers, the community is being transformed. This is a holistic program, where all the needs of children are being met: physical, mental, and spiritual. Children are discovering hope in Christ, who comes to them through the dedication and sacrifice of His people.

On a trip to Berlin, we visited the Kaiser Wilhelm Memorial Church, which has been turned into a war memorial. When workmen began rebuilding the church, which had been severely bombed, they found the statue of Christ badly damaged. When craftsmen began the process of restoration, one arm could not be found. So today, the statue stands at the altar with one arm missing as a reminder that we are the arms of Christ. Yes, Jesus goes into the most needy areas of the world through His followers. He uses our hands, feet, arms, and shoulders to continue His work.

And when we pray with the desperation of this mother, God will hear us.

In *Pilgrim's Progress* by John Bunyan, Christiana (the hero's wife), Mercy (a young pilgrim), and the children are graphically pictured knocking on Wicket Gate. They knock and knock, but no one answers. Meanwhile, a ferocious dog begins to bark—frightening the women and children. If they continue to knock, they fear the dog will attack. If they turn away, they fear the gatekeeper will be offended. They determine to knock again, ever so fervently. Finally, they hear the voice of the gatekeeper asking, "Who is there?" and the dog ceases barking.

Sometimes we are discouraged by God's silence and the obstacles that erode our confidence in His promises. The barking dogs should not discourage our faith, but make us all the more determined to draw near. "It is faith's work to claim and challenge loving kindness out of the roughest strokes of God."[4]

Based on what we have learned from this persistent mother, the following guide will also help you in approaching Jesus with your requests:

1. Humbly come to Him and acknowledge who He is.
2. Boldly ask for His mercy and help for a specific need.
3. Quietly accept His rebuke.
4. Persistently present your need.
5. Faithfully believe He will grant your request.

The silence of God should never be interpreted as indifference. Jesus stands ready to help the desperate and the persistent.

A PRAYER

Father, birth within me the faith of this woman, the persistent confidence that if I knock, You will answer, and if I seek, I will find. Help me not to give up in despair when I am discouraged, but to press on to receive the blessings and miracles that You wish to give me. Teach me humility of heart and determination of mind to believe that pursuing You is life's greatest joy and reward. In Jesus' name, Amen.

Now one of the Pharisees invited Jesus to have dinner with him, so he went to the Pharisee's house and reclined at the table. When a woman who had lived a sinful life in that town learned that Jesus was eating at the Pharisee's house, she brought an alabaster jar of perfume, and as she stood behind him at his feet weeping, she began to wet his feet with her tears. Then she wiped them with her hair, kissed them and poured perfume on them.

When the Pharisee who had invited him saw this, he said to himself, "If this man were a prophet, he would know who is touching him and what kind of woman she is—that she is a sinner."

Jesus answered him, "Simon, I have something to tell you."

"Tell me, teacher," he said.

"Two men owed money to a certain moneylender. One owed him five hundred denarii, and the other fifty. Neither of them had the money to pay him back, so he canceled the debts of both. Now which of them will love him more?"

Simon replied, "I suppose the one who had the bigger debt canceled."

"You have judged correctly," Jesus said.

Then he turned toward the woman and said to Simon, "Do you see this woman? I came into your house. You did not give me any water for my feet, but she wet my feet with her tears and wiped them with her hair. You did not give me a kiss, but this woman, from the time I entered, has not stopped kissing my feet. You did not put oil on my head, but she has poured perfume on my feet. Therefore, I tell you, her many sins have been forgiven—for she loved much. But he who has been forgiven little loves little."

Then Jesus said to her, "Your sins are forgiven."

The other guests began to say among themselves, "Who is this who even forgives sins?"

Jesus said to the woman, "Your faith has saved you; go in peace."   LUKE 7: 36-50

4

JESUS, LOVER OF A PROSTITUTE

Women become prostitutes for many different reasons. For some, prostitution seems to be the easiest way to survive because they believe there are few other options. For others, the choice is more deliberate.

This became evident to us when we were introduced to a woman we'll call Jamie. She had been adopted into a wealthy family where she experienced sexual abuse at an early age. The memories of what had happened stayed with her despite counseling she received in college. After graduating with honors, Jamie refused to return home, fearing that the abuse would continue. Cutting off all ties with her family, she began to travel to various cities, dancing in night clubs.

Lonely and insecure, Jamie looked to men for love and protection, not realizing that for them, love *was* sex. And protection, at best, usually lasted only for a night.

While in "the business," as she called it, Jamie became friends with a man who was in charge of the city vice squad. In exchange for sexual favors, he guaranteed that she would not be arrested. Now, rather than walking the streets, she parlayed her trade in exclusive hotels.

Through a stroke of providence, Jamie met a woman who had become a Christian. Together they came to the Moody Church, and Erwin gave Jamie a taped message on sexual healing.

She listened to the message repeatedly and cried out to God, but still could not find the strength to leave her profession. She was afraid to leave her lifestyle, thinking she did not have the abilities she needed to survive in the "straight world."

From Chicago, Jamie moved to a brothel in Nevada where prostitution was legal. Although she could justify what she was doing in her mind, her heart told her something quite different. She felt degraded, lonely, and sad. But still, she could not bring herself to leave her profession.

Finally, one day she reached the point where she simply could not take it anymore. In desperation, Jamie got on all fours and prayed aloud, "God, give me the strength to change my lifestyle . . . *make it impossible for me to continue doing this.*"

God heard her prayer of utter despair and He answered her. Although she had been converted earlier, Jamie finally *knew* that Christ had saved her, and that she was a daughter of God. Months later, she was baptized at the Moody Church, and today she is honorably employed. God has kept her morally pure, and thanks to Jesus, she has a bright future.

If you ask Jamie why she has been able to live without returning to immorality, she will tell you it is because of the Word of God. She reads the Bible daily, and with understanding. She also seeks wise counsel when making decisions. She is convinced she would not be alive today were it not for Jesus.

Jamie says that the same Jesus who spoke with love and compassion to the prostitute two thousand years ago still whispers the same words of forgiveness to such women today.

∞

We all know stories about people who have experienced more hurt than help in the presence of religious, judgmental people.

But Jesus had a habit of turning the tables by excoriating the religious types and showing mercy to the fallen. He issued forgiveness to those who sought it and a sharp rebuke to those who thought they didn't need such gifts from God. Grace for the needy and censure to the self-righteous was His pattern.

Nowhere do we see Jesus breaking with tradition as clearly as in the story about a prostitute who found healing in the house of a hypocrite. This woman was welcomed by Jesus in the very room where others scorned her. In the presence of Jesus, she received more understanding than the bystanders who longed to see her condemned.

Women keenly feel the pain that immorality brings. Some believe false promises; some are forced beyond their will; some betray their hearts; many just want to be loved. Jesus, known for reaching out to those who needed Him most, gave this woman a new identity and an inner peace. This should be an encouragement to all who are haunted by a sexual past.

Simon was a Pharisee who threw a feast for Christ because he wanted to check out this miracle worker for himself. Condescendingly, he invited Jesus to a dinner party at his house. According to custom, only men were invited. But in those days uninvited guests were welcome to stand along the walls of the room to listen to the theological discussion that took place after the meal. Evidently, this feast was well-publicized, and perhaps a number of such guests stopped by. That a woman would invite herself was in itself in bad taste; that she should be a woman of the street made this socially intolerable.

The visitors were seated at a low table, perhaps a foot higher than the floor. Each of the guests would recline at the table, leaning toward his left, propped up by his left arm, and free to eat with his right hand. We have reason to believe that according to custom, Jesus, as the prominent invited guest, was given a place of honor.

The unwelcome woman is described as having lived a sinful life. Since all people are sinners, it is clear that the writer Luke wants us to understand that this woman was a sinner of a special sort, namely, an immoral woman. Almost certainly she was a prostitute, a woman who was known to have had countless sexual relationships.

There are reasons why women fall into such a lifestyle. Often, a woman who has been abused or molested feels shameful and unworthy of the love and acceptance of a faithful husband. She feels safer in the arms of a man who will use her for his own selfish desires. Emotionally devastated, she believes that a life on the streets is her only option. On the other hand, a young woman brought up in a fine home may rebel, become influenced by the wrong crowd, and experiment with sex, drugs, and alcohol. She leaves home falsely believing that her life is ruined. Homeless and penniless, she thinks her only option is prostitution.

Sometimes a woman is seduced by a man in the workplace, who sooner or later leaves her for someone else. She feels rejected and humiliated. As the years pass, one relationship leads to another until she feels used and worthless. Eventually, she decides to sell her body to make a living.

Perhaps this woman who came to Jesus was betrayed and abandoned by her husband, so she turned to the only profession that would bring in money. The men she hated could be used for a few shekels, allowing her to survive on the streets. "She allowed herself to be passed from man to man like a dirty magazine, seized eagerly, used briefly then thrown aside."[1]

As she approached Jesus, the woman spoke no words of apology or explanation. Acting as though they were the only ones in the room, she proceeded with her planned ceremony.

She knelt behind Him and from within her robe, produced an expensive bottle of perfume. She opened the vial and began to pour its precious contents on Jesus' extended feet. As the lovely fragrance filled the room, she began to weep. The tears poured down her cheeks, and in a moment Jesus' feet were drenched; in fact, the Greek phrase could be translated that "she began to rain on his feet with her tears." Then she wiped His soaked feet with her hair. This act of devotion was done repeatedly, unashamedly.

Simon was offended. He feared that his well-planned dinner party might be ruined. What annoyed him the most was that his honored guest had not reacted according to custom. "All of the rules of etiquette dictated that Jesus should have recoiled in horror at being touched by so loathsome a creature."[2] This, in Simon's mind, was proof that Jesus was not a prophet, for if He was, He would have known who this woman was and her occupation, too. How could Jesus allow her to act so disgracefully and even be a willing participant in her disgusting outburst of affection?

The whole atmosphere was charged with contempt for this woman who had the audacity to defy established custom and disrupt a classy feast. Simon was embarrassed, even if Christ wasn't. So much for the planned topic of discussion for the evening.

Here is this woman in the presence of both Christ and a Pharisee; the one accepts her and the other resents her. In the end, the Lord of Glory told her that her sins were forgiven. What more could an immoral woman ask?

FROM SHAME TO PEACE

What an incredible story. Her tears cleansed the feet of the most perfect man on earth; His forgiveness cleansed the soul of the most sinful woman in town! She instantly made the transition from self-loathing to peace when Jesus forgave her and restored her dignity. Thanks to Him, she was able to do in a few moments what others cannot accomplish on their own in a lifetime.

What are those qualities that enabled this woman to receive Jesus' attention and mercy?

She was honest. This woman had no desire for hypocrisy or pretense. She knew that coming to the house of a self-righteous Pharisee would elicit derision and scorn. But her longing for a new life overcame her natural inclination to hide her shame. Her desire to meet Christ was more powerful than her fear of the moral ridicule she would receive from Simon the chauvinist and his friends. Given the culture of the day, she had no reason to expect grace; the religious types knew only how to execute the harsh penalties of the law.

The grace of God works in our lives when we honestly expose our hidden sin in God's presence. The first step toward breaking the power of an immoral past as someone once said is "to die to the natural inclination to live a lie." God's grace and help comes to those who are weary of their sinful secrets, and who ask for forgiveness and cleansing. We are assured in Romans 5:20 that where sin abounds, grace abounds much more. God sends His grace to deliver us from our sin.

We do not have to change ourselves in order to be worthy of coming to Jesus. We must simply come as we are, openly, honestly, expectantly. "He who conceals his transgressions will not prosper, but he who confesses and forsakes them will find compassion" (Proverbs 28:13, NASB).

You must be willing to face your past in the presence of Jesus. He can heal your brokenness and bring peace to your soul. He replaces defilement with wholeness, and emptiness with peace.

She had faith. We're surprised by this woman's faith. She believed whatever she had heard about Jesus. Perhaps it was the kindness on His face or maybe she had listened at a distance to His messages of love and hope. And there in His presence, her faith blossomed; she knew that this man could be trusted, unlike so many others who had used her.

She anointed Him, believing He would accept her despite the fact that He knew all about her. In return He said to her, "Your faith has saved you; go in peace" (Luke 7:50). Her tears did not save her, nor did the loving act of pouring expensive perfume on His feet. Her good deeds did not bring the salvation of God to her soul. Faith, and faith alone, in Jesus' forgiveness and salvation wiped her sins away.

How thankful she was that Jesus was not a Pharisee. Imagine if He had said to her, "Woman, I don't appreciate being touched by a prostitute. Don't you know that I am the Holy Son of God? Go back to the streets where you belong!" If she had been rejected by the only One qualified to forgive her, there was no other place in the universe where she might go to be forgiven. If the Son of God turned His back, she would have been forced to walk away in eternal despair. But since He spoke a word of forgiveness, she left His presence with eternal joy.

She confronted her feelings. Why was this woman weeping? Think of the men who betrayed her. False assurances of love and broken promises. Her self-worth had long since been stripped away. Maybe she remembered that a family had been ruined because of the sin she committed with the father and husband of the home. Or perhaps she had children of her own who were being neglected because of her lifestyle. She may also have wept from the grief of a broken heart.

The tears of a lifetime ran down her cheeks and fell onto

Jesus' feet. The present tense of the verbs indicates that she kept on weeping, kept on anointing, kept on wiping His feet with her hair. The pain in her life—guilt, shame, rejection, defilement, failure—came pouring out.

She could have taken all of these feelings and stuffed them deep within her soul, unwilling to face the pain of the past. But she would have become a bitter woman, defiant and angry. Or she could have simply pursued continuous compulsive relationships to deaden the pain of an empty life. She could have continued to run from one relationship to another, never admitting the fruitlessness of her search for love and self-worth.

People who struggle with a history of sexual brokenness often have a moment of truth, a time when they are finally willing to confront the pain that has been pushed down into the depths of their soul.

Weeping often accompanies repentance. This doesn't mean that we cannot be forgiven unless we weep, nor does it mean that this woman's tears paid for her misdeeds. But sexual sin almost always involves deep pain that is hidden to others. For every illicit relationship there is another layer of hurt.

It is said that children who have been abused have "no place in the depths of their soul where they may cry their eyes out."

God has given us tear ducts so we can release painful feelings and memories. Healing begins when we are willing to let our tears flow in the presence of Jesus.

She accepted forgiveness. Jesus set the agenda of the discussion that evening. We've already learned that Simon believed that if Jesus had truly been a prophet, He would not have allowed this woman to touch Him. Since Jesus let her touch Him, in Simon's mind, this was proof that Jesus was a crude rabbi who did not have the decency to follow the custom of the day. Simon rejected Jesus' actions, so he rejected Jesus Himself. Simon thought he knew what God would do if He were in Jesus' shoes.

Jesus revealed Simon's heart by telling this parable. "'Two men owed money to a certain moneylender. One owed him five hundred denarii, and the other fifty. Neither of them had the money to pay him back, so he canceled the debts of both. Now which of them will love him more?' Simon replied, 'I suppose the one who had the bigger debt canceled'"(vv. 41-43).

Then Jesus brought His point home. "Do you see this woman? I came into your house. You did not give me any water for my feet, but she wet my feet with her tears and wiped them with her hair. You did not give me a kiss, but this woman, from the time I entered, has not stopped kissing my feet. You did not put oil on my head, but she has poured perfume on my feet. Therefore, I tell you, her many sins have been forgiven—for she loved much. But he who has been forgiven little loves little" (vv. 44-47).

The story hit its mark.

Imagine the look that must have come over Simon's face when Jesus told this tale, revealing His host's self-righteous thoughts. By showing Simon that He knew what he was thinking, Jesus proved by inference that yes, He knew who touched Him and yes, He was a prophet after all. In fact, He was a prophet who not only knew this woman's past, but He was also qualified to give her the promise of a new future.

Let's not hurry over Jesus' words, "Do you see this woman?" What He was asking was, "Do you *really* see her for what she is? Can you see someone who needs help and someone who needs grace?" Jesus showed the contrast between this woman and the Pharisee. Simon needed forgiveness as much as this woman, probably even more so. People who know they need forgiveness are closer to the Kingdom than those who do not think they need such mercy. That is why Jesus said that the prostitutes go to heaven ahead of the self-righteous folk.

The tension in the room was palpable as Jesus made the point that the degree of our love depends on the degree of our forgiveness. Of course this should not be interpreted to mean that since Simon had seemingly few sins that needed forgiveness, he could never love Christ deeply. Christ's intent was to teach that those who *think* they need little forgiveness love only little. Those who see their sin clearly will love much.

Who was Simon to make judgments against others when he also had failed? Self-satisfied, he regarded others with contempt. His self-deceit was so well hidden even to himself, that he could not see reality in any other way. This woman saw *her* sin and Simon saw her sin, but he could not see his own. As a result, he was unable to love. *He was on good terms with himself but on bad terms with God.*

But in the presence of this self-righteous, judgmental bigot and his friends, Jesus declares for all to hear, "Your sins are forgiven" (v. 48). Perhaps for the first time in years, someone actually spoke to her in kindness; someone gave her the dignity of letting those around her know that she was special to God. She was validated as having worth.

Sometimes people who have committed sexual sins feel too unworthy to be forgiven. Yes, we are all unworthy, but God's grace is all one-sided; we bring nothing to the table except our great need. Forgiveness is a free gift based upon the merit of Jesus. That's why God does not find it more difficult to forgive big sins than He does lesser ones.

It is God's will that you be totally cleared of the guilt of your sin regardless of the awful consequences it has produced. If David could be forgiven for adultery and for having Uriah killed (who could never be raised back to life), we can be sure that God will also forgive sexual sin despite its ongoing consequences.

She accepted cleansing. Many people who accept the forgiveness of Jesus still struggle with lingering guilt and self-condemnation. A young woman once wrote us saying that an older woman had convinced her they should have a sexual relationship. Although initially resistant, she gave in, beginning a five-year struggle with lesbianism. "Oh, how I stink in the core of my being!" she wrote. "I know God has forgiven me, but I cannot forgive myself. Many times I cannot help but cry . . . I feel so tired and old. Is there any hope for someone like me? God forbid that I should be a Judas, who felt sorry for what he had done, but nevertheless chose to go in the wrong direction!"

Yes! A thousand times yes—there is hope.

But why does this letter writer still feel defiled even though she has confessed her sins, perhaps many times? First, she must not only claim God's forgiveness, but also God's cleansing, which is her right. Her conscience can be wiped clean, and she can live without the voices of condemnation, without the heaviness that comes with a defiled conscience. "If we confess our sins, he is faithful and righteous to forgive us our sins and to cleanse us from all unrighteousness" (1 John 1:9, NASB).

Second, she may be making the error of confusing the accusations of the devil with the voice of the Holy Spirit. The responsibility of the Holy Spirit is to convict us of sin so that we might confess it, and after that, the Spirit brings peace to our hearts. Sometimes at that point Satan takes over and tries to imitate the work of God, convicting us of sins that God has already forgiven. Believers who think the accusations of the devil are the convictions of the Spirit are caught in a vicious cycle of continual confession without the assurance of forgiveness. Or they believe the lie that they must live with guilt as a payment for sin.

Forgiveness and cleansing are available for every shameful sexual sin. No sin is too great to be forgiven. Wallowing in guilt will not pay for our sin. The death of Jesus—the death He was to die after He forgave this woman in Simon's home—that death and resurrection would pay for her sin and for ours, too.

If you have confessed your sin, the next time Satan reminds you of your past, remind him of his future. He has, after all, been defeated by Christ's death and resurrection, and thus eternal judgment awaits him.

There are those who cannot forgive themselves. If the Supreme Lawgiver of the universe has pronounced you clean, do you have the right to pronounce yourself dirty? God takes our forgiven sin and throws it into the depths of the sea, remembering it no more. Must we live with remorse? The answer is no, for remorse is simply repentance made out of Jesus' sight. But when we come before Him, the conscience is made clean and the guilt is transferred to our crucified Redeemer.

If a prostitute could believe while in the presence of Jesus two thousand years ago, then a lesbian can believe today. Both can hear the voice of the Savior, "Your sins are forgiven." Resist the temptation to come to Jesus with something in your hand, some promise of reform, some act of penitence that you intend to do. Come just as you are. Bring your darkness into His light.

THE WALK TO FREEDOM

Christ's final words to this woman were, "Go in peace" (v. 50). Forgiveness is always accompanied by peace. It was as if Jesus threw open the gates to a fresh garden. For her as for us, there is a promise of new life that we can enter with joy. She is given a clean slate, a second chance at life. To "go" meant that from that moment forward she would be a different woman with a different lifestyle. The Lord who forgave her was also the Lord who would empower her to live a new life.

Sometimes drastic measures have to be taken to break free

from the chains of the past. When speaking of lust and adultery, Jesus said, "If your right eye causes you to sin, gouge it out and throw it away. It is better for you to lose one part of your body than for your whole body to be thrown into hell. And if your right hand causes you to sin, cut if off and throw it away. It is better for you to lose one part of your body than for your whole body to go into hell" (Matthew 5:29–30). Jesus is saying in the strongest possible language, "Do whatever you have to do so that you will not keep sliding into the pit of sexual sin." That includes forgiving those who have wronged you and becoming accountable to those who can help you stand against past behavioral patterns.

We should all be memorizing promises from the Bible and standing in the completeness of God's forgiveness. Faith in the power of the Word of God gives us the strength we need to live differently. The Holy Spirit is with all those who desire to walk in a new path.

Remember, we will always be tempted to return to the sin that once was our master. We must learn to resist Satan and enlist others who will pray against his power. The battle will rage but victory is possible through Jesus Christ our Lord.

Charles Wesley understood that many people still struggle against the very sins that have been canceled by God. But he assures us:

> He breaks the power of cancelled sin
> He sets the prisoner free
> His blood can make the foulest clean
> His blood availed for me

Thousands of people, once plagued by a sexual past, are walking in freedom today, thanks to the power of Jesus' blood. They have been set free from prisons of guilt, bitterness, anger, self-loathing, and hatred. Jesus broke these chains for all of us, if we are willing to come to Him as this woman did so many years ago. The past cannot be changed, but the *power* of the past can be diminished and broken.

A PRAYER

Heavenly Father, I bring all that I am into Your presence, through Jesus our Lord. You know my past, my pain, and my secrets. I open my life to You, asking for Your forgiveness and cleansing. Today I confess that Jesus is both the Redeemer of my past and the Lord of my future. By faith I accept His pronouncement that He is my righteousness, and I am clean. Thank You for His love and acceptance. I pray in His name, Amen.

One of the synagogue rulers, named Jairus, came there. Seeing Jesus, he fell at his feet and pleaded earnestly with him, "My little daughter is dying. Please come and put your hands on her so that she will be healed and live." . . .

A large crowd followed and pressed around him. And a woman was there who had been subject to bleeding for twelve years. She had suffered a great deal under the care of many doctors and had spent all she had, yet instead of getting better she grew worse. When she heard about Jesus, she came up behind him in the crowd and touched his cloak, because she thought, "If I just touch his clothes, I will be healed." Immediately her bleeding stopped and she felt in her body that she was freed from her suffering.

MARK 5:22-29

5

JESUS, LOVER OF
THE SICK AND THE DYING

God does not always give us the answers to our prayers that we ask for. Often, He does not deliver us from our trials, but instead gives us the grace to go through them.

For more than forty years, I (Rebecca) have suffered from terrible headaches. Throbbing, excruciating pain! More than half of that time, the headaches were relieved only mildly by the medications I had available. Some would last three to four days, accompanied by horrible pain and vomiting. In the late 1980s, I underwent an extensive evaluation at a well-known headache clinic, and finally discovered that my malady had a name—migraines. I was given a variety of drugs, with little success. Some of the pills, injections, and patches caused debilitating side effects. And some didn't work at all.

All aspects of my life have been affected by these headaches: studying, working as a nurse, serving in ministry, traveling, and caring for my family. At times, my family has even gathered around me and prayed for relief and deliverance. My dear husband has interceded on my behalf many times, begging God to have mercy on me. His compassion, concern, and prayers have been comforting and encouraging. God's grace and strength gave me the determination and tenacity to keep going in spite of the pain. In the early nineties, a new drug came onto the market that for me was life changing. How miraculous to be able to take a small pill and have my headache disappear in just one hour, rather than seventy-two or more. I have tearfully thanked God often for this amazing medication.

Occasionally, however, even this drug doesn't work, especially with a left-sided migraine. During such an occasion in the summer of 2003, I had several days of cluster headaches—one after another with only a few hours of relief in between. I had been planning a trip to Colorado to spend some time in my beloved mountains and to visit friends. In spite of the pain I was experiencing, I decided to stick to my plans. As I drove into the mountains that night in the rental car, the stress of a long day of flying and the higher elevation enhanced the pounding pain in my head. After settling into my accommodations, I faced a long night of agony—the medication wasn't working and I felt desperate.

For a couple of hours, I lay very still with an ice pack on my head. But there was no relief and the pain was frightening. When it seemed that my head would explode, I cried out in fear and pain, asking my heavenly Father whether He cared. When would this nightmare end? There was no one to pray for me, to comfort and encourage me. In the darkness and loneliness of my room, I cried out to Jesus to have mercy on me. As the tears spilled from my eyes, I reached out my arm toward Him. For a moment, I believed that if only I could touch the hem of His garment, surely I would be made whole. With great faith, I extended my hand, expecting a miracle. The throbbing in my temple continued.

But—and I remember this so vividly—the presence and peace of Jesus filled the room. A feeling of calm came over me, and the grace that He promises in our time of need was there. In a few moments, I fell into a deep sleep. When I awoke a couple of hours later, the intense throbbing had subsided. I took more medication and was able to go back to sleep. When I awoke in the morning, my head was clear—for the first time in several days.

No, I was not healed that night, but I did experience a divine encounter with Jesus. His peace, power, and presence gave me the grace and ability to go through my trial without losing faith in His love and plan for me.

The story of the bleeding woman has always been a favorite of mine. I see myself in her—filled with fear, doubt, and a sense of hopelessness, wondering whether Jesus cares. But thankfully, this woman teaches us that we can come to Jesus as we are, reach out, and accept His mercy by faith. She has often been my inspiration to leave the shadows and walk in the sunshine of Jesus' love and acceptance.

Jesus asks us to step out of our comfort zones and come to Him just as this woman did. He walks with us through our pain and trials. He knows our limits. He tests our faith. He calls us "daughters." The One who walked the dusty streets of Jerusalem is here to help us in our desperation and personal need. A miracle may take place when we reach out in faith to touch the hem of His garment.

ᏜᏜ

Today we often read about what women want, what their needs are, and how their struggle for fulfillment and recognition is jeopardized by the expectations of society and culture. But truth be told, these challenges have been with us since the beginning of human existence. Times have changed, but suffering has not.

When we reach back, we find continuity with those who have gone before us. "Yet in reality, women today, despite their freedom, experience all the same things as did their sisters down through the centuries. Our newfound freedoms have not alleviated loneliness, shame, failure, and heartbreak."[1] If the surveys are to be believed, many women are unhappy, feeling that life has cheated them of their potential. Either because of personal failure, the actions of others, or the constraints of society, they have had to come to terms with deep disappointment.

We know of a woman who has suffered from multiple sclerosis for many years and lives with an impatient husband who often reminds her that she is a financial and emotional drain he can scarcely tolerate. Their children are grown and the youngest is about to leave for college. She dreads the day when she will be alone, left to contemplate her fate and the guilt she feels for being a burden that no one wants to bear.

Similar feelings would have haunted this woman who met Jesus two thousand years ago, a woman who lived in the shadows until she came into the light of Jesus' power and grace. She was not only sick, she was also struggling in a culture rooted in religious and cultural taboos that restricted her social contacts. She would never have received a sympathetic ear from the leaders of her synagogue. Her physical disability was only a part of the problem. Being ostracized from society and living with her painful secret was the greater issue, a pain that drove her to despair.

And then she encountered Jesus.

Jesus met this woman while He was on His way to perform another miracle, answering the cry of a father whose daughter was on the verge of death. Let's consider the context: As the popularity of Jesus grew, crowds around Him became increasingly demanding and often unruly. At the word of Jesus, a demonized man was returned to his senses, but when the demons entered a herd of pigs and they drowned, Jesus was asked to leave the territory of the Gerasenes, which was on the east side of Galilee.

One crowd sighed with relief when Jesus left, but another

was waiting to welcome Him. A father had an urgent need: his twelve-year-old daughter was near death. "One of the synagogue rulers, named Jairus, came there. Seeing Jesus, he fell at his feet and pleaded earnestly with him, 'My little daughter is dying. Please come and put hands on her so that she will be healed and live'" (Mark 5:22-23). So Jesus started for the man's house and the crowd followed.

But then the journey was interrupted.

THE WOMAN WITH CONTINUAL BLEEDING

A woman saw that Jesus was in her vicinity and decided to take advantage of what might be her one and only opportunity. Faith overcame her fear. Hope overcame her weakness. Soon Jesus would pass by and she would be waiting for Him.

Here we see the contrast between the urgent need of a critically ill child, and the long-standing need of a chronically ill woman for whom there was no cure. A closer look reveals another contrast: the sick child was the daughter of a prominent synagogue ruler, while the sick woman was an insignificant member of society who had found no help from the medical establishment. However, there was one interesting similarity between the child and the woman: for every year the girl had lived—twelve—the woman had been bleeding.

Most of us don't like interruptions. The anxious father was in a hurry for Jesus to get to his house before his daughter died. But unknown to Jairus and the demanding throng, Jesus lived by a divinely appointed schedule. As the large crowd pressed around Him, pleading for His help, there was *one* who needed Him more than all the others. What would Jesus do? The earthly father willed that Jesus heal *his* daughter; the heavenly Father willed that Jesus heal *His* "daughter."

Jairus was an important synagogue officer and this woman was an anonymous "nobody," yet Jesus stopped to help her. Jairus was wealthy, but this dear woman had nothing. Jairus was in a hurry, yet Jesus made him wait for a woman whose healing could probably have been postponed.

Yet on that day *both* Jairus and the woman would receive Jesus' help.

Her condition We might be able to imagine a menstrual flow that would last one month. Six months. One year—perhaps. Five years—maybe. But not twelve long years. And this wasn't just a flow; all three Gospel accounts refer to it as continual bleeding. The Greek word used can be translated *hemorrhage.* We can scarcely contemplate such a curse befalling any woman. And she had to deal with this kind of affliction without the convenience of modern day toiletries or sanitation. Unthinkable!

The implications were staggering. This woman was subject to the Levitical teaching that women were to be essentially quarantined during their menstrual flow. One passage speaks directly to her situation, "When a woman has a discharge of blood for many days at a time other than her monthly period or has a discharge that continues beyond her period, she will be unclean as long as she has the discharge, just as in the days of her period" (Leviticus 15:25). This uncleanness was not moral or physical, but ceremonial. It was God's way of reminding people of the reality of sin and disease.

Not only was she an unclean woman, but everything she touched became unclean. The clothes she wore. The bed she slept in. The furniture she sat on. It gets worse. "And whoever touches these things shall be unclean, and shall wash his clothes, and bathe himself in water, and be unclean until the evening" (Leviticus 15:27). Everyone who touched her or touched what she touched was unclean. They would have to wash themselves to restore their ceremonial purity.

Most likely, she was unmarried, for no husband would stay with a continually unclean wife. "A 'flow of blood' effectively meant that a woman could not leave home, not have intercourse with her husband or any normal social contact, much less any religious activity. In effect, this woman has been excluded by her society for twelve years."[2] There was also much superstition in those days about the causes of incurable illness—it was often attributed to a sin that had been committed, evil spirits, bad parents, or bad genes. No doubt, she was considered bad luck, and rarely left her place of dwelling. She must have felt like a leper. Or possibly like a person with AIDS, as when the disease was first discovered and thought to be communicable through ordinary contact. Evidently, the gynecologists of the day were baffled, though they were glad to accept her money.

In Mark's account, we discover deliberate irony, "She had suffered a great deal under the care of many doctors and had spent all she had, yet instead of getting better she grew worse" (5:26). Mark makes the point that all the physicians could do was add to her suffering. He implies that the physicians bungled her case badly. We can hardly imagine what some of their ancient cures might have been.

And if we read between the lines, it's even possible that she had been embarrassed many times by the professional jokes of these doctors or humiliated by their vulgar innuendos. When her resources ran out, her hope also ran out. Since no one would hire her, we can only wonder how she survived. Perhaps she received a few monthly coins from a charity, or there may have been a temple fund that helped the disabled. We do know that she probably lived far below the poverty line.

Anemic. Incurable. Destitute. Untouchable. Isolated. Lonely. Unloved.

But this woman never gave up hope. She refused to succumb to her illness, to become bedridden—an invalid. She would keep searching for a cure. She would keep praying for a miracle.

Then she heard of Jesus.

Occasionally, she visited the marketplace, shrouded in a hooded robe. Whispers about this amazing man reached her ears as she carefully moved from booth to booth. He didn't sound like the common rabbi. He didn't embarrass or shame women. He delivered people from evil spirits and demons. He was an incredible teacher who expounded the Scriptures. Crowds sought to touch Him, power came out from Him, and He healed many people (Luke 6:18-19).

Apparently, this was a man who was willing to disrupt the status quo by delivering people from cruel diseases and evil oppression. He was willing to risk making enemies by liberating women from centuries of repression and pious tradition. She would take advantage of His kindness.

Her plan Getting near Jesus was a risky venture. Many others would be pressing close to Him for a word of wisdom or for a healing touch. Jesus, she thought, would never know that someone "touched the *edge* of his cloak" (Luke 8:44, emphasis added). She feared her presence might cause a commotion and incur the wrath of His friends. She dared to touch Him, though only the "hem of his garment." The reference is to tassels that were worn by Jewish men as required by law (Deuteronomy 22:12). Touching the tassels on His robe meant that she understood what they stood for—the Torah, the law given by Moses. This part of the robe was regarded as most holy.

No one knew of her plan. Custom being what it was, decorum would have decreed that she not approach Jesus without a male escort. To walk behind and touch the fringe of His garment seemed innocuous, and she was probably hoping that no one would notice. She planned to quickly disappear into the crowd and hurry home to see if a miracle had happened.

Her touch, of course, would make Him unclean. But perhaps, she reasoned, if He had the power to heal her, He also had the power to remove any contamination she might pass on. It was a chance she had to take. She had nothing to give Jesus, no token of appreciation, no gift to express her gratefulness. Only the faith to believe that Jesus could and would heal her.

So the plan was in place. *I won't ask for anything; I won't speak to Him, or even let Him see me . . . but if I can just touch the edge of His cloak, maybe I'll get well.* She was at the right place at the right moment.

We are reminded of Mother Teresa and Princess Diana, who were not afraid to hold the hands of lepers and embrace people with AIDS. Sometimes we bypass an opportunity to comfort a sick and hurting person because we fear catching their illness.

Her healing When the woman reached out her hand and brushed the hem of Jesus' robe, her bleeding stopped immediately and "the flow of her blood was dried up" (Mark 5:29, NASB). Physiologically, something in her body changed—it was so definite that she *felt* it happen. This was a measurable, verifiable miracle. She knew that it was not the robe itself that healed her, but the person who wore it.

Imagine for a moment that you had experienced the same pathology for twelve years. Whether a headache, toothache, backache, abdominal pain, a broken arm, an oozing wound—you pick the affliction. When it stopped, you would know it. This woman *knew* instantly that she was healed of her disease. She probably wanted to shout: "Praise be to God!" But for fear of being rebuked, she silently shrank back into the crowd, according to plan.

But Jesus was well aware that this woman was in the crowd. He also knew He had been touched, not just by the crowd, but also by a special hand that sought His healing. He responded by allowing His power to go out to heal her. She could not have been healed without His knowledge and consent, nor could she magically steal power from Him. *Her touch could not make Him unclean; however, it would make her clean.*

When Jesus asked who touched Him, the disciples thought it was a ridiculous question, since the crowd was pressing around Him. What is more, if anyone had intentionally touched Him, they would have by now disappeared into the crowd.

But Jesus knew that someone had touched Him, not because He felt it physically, but because He sensed that "power had gone out from him" (Mark 5:30). Power equals energy or strength. The King James Version of the Bible describes it as *virtue*, which means something of exquisite worth and value. By no means was Jesus' strength depleted, as He responded to a touch made in faith.

When Mark says, "She had suffered a great deal," he uses a word for *suffering* that is only used here and then later describing the sufferings of Jesus Himself (vv. 26; cf. 8:31, 9:12). Perhaps as Jesus thought about her, He acknowledged that this woman had experienced in a small way what He Himself would endure in the months ahead. The suffering servant, as Jesus is called in Isaiah, personally identified with this hurting woman.

The woman knew she had been discovered. "But the woman, knowing what had happened to her, came in fear and trembling and fell down before him and told him the whole truth" (Mark 5:33, ESV). Her attitude and posture shows she was well aware that she had overstepped the bounds of protocol. But Jesus did not shame her for violating religious and cultural customs. Indeed, by speaking to her publicly, He broke with enforced rabbinical social taboos.

Why did He identify her publicly?

He called her forth to encourage her in the presence of others. He wanted everyone within earshot to hear her story—illness, suffering, healing—from her own lips. "He called her forth from her hiding place and confirmed her as a person."[3]

A public healing. A public testimony.

He also called her forth to restore her place in society. "Having healed her, now He could help her reclaim her identity in the community and glorify God in the process."[4] There would be no doubt that she was now clean.

He spoke kindly, lovingly, endearingly: "*Daughter.*" This is the only time Jesus is recorded as using this word that included her as a member of His spiritual family. "Daughter, your faith has healed you. Go in peace and be freed from your suffering" (v. 34). Her faith had made her well, and she became a member of God's family in the process. Those who stood around were amazed that this woman, so low on the social scale, received such validation and affirmation from the master Teacher and Healer.

Jesus also brought the health of forgiveness to her soul. She was to "go in peace." Her search was over, her suffering had ended, and her soul could now be at rest. Jesus left her fully restored, body and soul.

In our home we receive many periodicals and magazines that focus on good health. In them is a wealth of knowledge about diets, exercise, and nutritional supplements. But unfortunately, they contain no information on how to make the soul healthier. Yet Jesus spoke about the relative value of the soul and body when He said, "Do not be afraid of those who kill the body but cannot kill the soul. Rather, be afraid of the One who can destroy both soul and body in hell" (Matthew 10:28). This body will eventually die, whether we are healed or not; whether we follow the latest nutritional advice or not. In contrast, the soul continues for all of eternity, either in glory or agony.

Scripture records just two miracles that occurred that day. Surely, many other people touched Jesus, but we don't know if anyone else received a miracle. Perhaps their desires or motives were wrong. Perhaps He was testing them. Jesus, knowing every human heart, made the decision. This woman was distinguished for three reasons: she was desperate, she wanted to be healed, and she believed. "It is one thing to throng Him, and quite something else to trust Him."[5]

Jesus honored her focused faith. Though fearful and forgotten, she attracted the attention of the only One who could help her. Hers was a case of physical bleeding, but many women today bleed psychologically and spiritually. Family, friends, and spiritual advisors may have tried to help, but those who are hurting have only gotten worse. Their wounds have never healed. Year after year they hemorrhage emotionally. For them, as for this dear woman, their only hope is Jesus.

And what about those who are not healed physically, although they seek it as eagerly as this woman in Luke? Joni Eareckson Tada is a quadriplegic as the result of a diving accident in 1967. She was encouraged to seek healing by reading books and attending faith-healing services. The passage she claimed for herself was the promise Jesus gave to the invalid next to the Pool of Bethesda. Jesus said to him matter of factly, "Get up! Pick up your mat and walk" (John 5:8). And the man was healed.

Despite her countless prayers and presence at faith-healing services, Joni was never healed. Thirty years later she visited Israel and the Pool of Bethesda. There, she thanked God that He did not answer her prayers for healing. "I thanked God," she said, "because I would never have experienced His nearness as I have in this wheelchair for the past thirty years."

Not all of us are healed physically and emotionally when we come to Jesus. But we are all helped. Our souls are restored and our hope of heaven is confirmed. Jesus speaks to all who suffer today and says, "I want *you* as my daughter." The invitation to join His family is given to all.

No one who encounters Jesus ever remains the same. Here is His promise:

"Come to me, all you who are weary and burdened, and I will give you rest. Take my yoke upon you and learn from me, for I am gentle and humble in heart, and you will find rest for your souls. For my yoke is easy and my burden is light" (Matthew 11:28-30). To those who reach out in faith, Jesus is there to comfort, to strengthen, and to give the assurance of His presence.

For Jesus there are no crowds, just individuals with specific names, faces, and needs.

THE DAUGHTER WHO DIED

Possibly another reason why Jesus interacted publicly with the restored woman was to encourage the faith of Jairus who was still at His side. It was not easy for this ruler of a synagogue to come to Jesus. Jesus said and did much to offend the Pharisees, those who occupied the synagogues and taught the law. In fact, he had even been accused of blasphemy and being in cahoots with the darker side of the underworld by this group of religious leaders.

No doubt Jairus had sought the help and wisdom of the most highly recommended physicians for his daughter. But he was a desperate parent. Better to incur the wrath and sarcasm of his colleagues than to forgo the opportunity to witness the power of

Jesus. His daughter was dying; what others thought simply did not matter.

The account is dramatic. While Jesus was speaking the words, "Go in peace," to the newly healed woman, "someone from the ruler's house came and said, 'Your daughter is dead; do not trouble the Teacher any more' " (Luke 8:49, ESV).

What crushing news!

"Ignoring what they said, Jesus told the synagogue ruler, 'Don't be afraid; just believe' " (Mark 5:36). Now Jairus was faced with an option: should he believe the words of the messenger or should he believe the words of Jesus? He had exercised some faith by coming to Jesus, and now Jesus was encouraging him to "keep believing." Of course, it was easier for him to trust Jesus when his daughter was alive. Death has such finality; to raise a sick child to health is one thing, to raise a child from the dead is quite another. If only Jesus had hurried, rather than spending time with the woman who interrupted His journey.

But for Jesus there are no interruptions, only divine appointments. He planned to do an even bigger miracle for Jairus than He did for the woman.

"*Ignoring what they said . . .*" (v. 36).

There is a wealth of wisdom in those words. We must at times ignore both the comments and the advice of those who would lead us astray. The voice we listen to determines the direction we walk.

Let us agree to *ignore* condemning words, belittling words, and discouraging words. Words of an angry parent or spouse or friend. Negative words. Sarcastic words. Faithless words that cannot see God in any difficult circumstance. Words of unbelief and condemnation. Such words have the power to damage our souls.

Jairus was not only devastated by the news of his daughter's death, but also by the fact that the mourning customs were already beginning. Jesus asks for the cause of the lamentation.

"'Why all this commotion and wailing? The child is not dead but asleep.' But they laughed at him" (vv. 39-40).

Why would Jesus say that the girl was sleeping, when in fact, the child was dead? Jesus uses the word *sleep*, not because the soul sleeps, as some have thought, but because the body sleeps until the day of resurrection. The soul or spirit goes to God in heaven, but the body sleeps and shall be awakened in the last day.

Jesus said the same of Lazarus. "Our friend Lazarus has fallen asleep; but I am going there to wake him up" (John 11:11). We've all had times when we fall into bed, bone weary and grateful for a time of sleep. We do not fear sleeping, for we are confident that we shall awake rejuvenated. Just so, when we die, we need not fear, for in the end we will be awakened by the word of Jesus. In His presence the dead are but sleeping, awaiting resurrection.

Jesus' point was that this girl was not in a permanent state of death; she was "sleeping," and He was going to wake her up, not on the final day of resurrection, but right *then.* The reason the people who surrounded Jesus laughed is because they did not understand who was standing in their midst. In the presence of Jesus, there are no impossibilities.

Jesus, not wanting to make the miracle a spectacle, insisted that everyone else wait outside as He took the child's parents and the disciples into her room. Mark could not get the original expression that Jesus used out of his mind. So he preserved the original Aramaic and then translated for his Greek readers. We read, "He took her by the hand and said to her, '*Talitha koum!*' (which means, 'Little girl, I say to you, get up!'). Immediately the girl stood up and walked around. . . . At this they were completely astonished" (Mark 5:41-42).

And well might they be!

We see the contrast between the despair of the mourners and the hope that Jesus brought. The bearers of the bad news said

Jesus was too late, but Jesus always arrives on time, in accordance with the divine plan. No matter how hopeless the situation, He speaks the words of comfort and power. Jesus was calm and controlled while the crowd was weeping out of control.

We've seen the difference between a family that has trusted Jesus and one that has not, as we have stood at a coffin in a funeral home. For one there is hope in the midst of tears; for the other, there is mourning without comfort. No wonder Paul wrote that we should not "grieve like the rest of men, who have no hope" (1 Thessalonians 4:13). The pagans said of the early Christians, "They carry their dead as if in triumph."

We can even face death confidently in the presence of Jesus. "The worst human disaster can be met with courage and gallantry when we meet it with God. They laughed him to scorn because they thought that his hope was groundless and his calm mistaken."[6]

These two stories are a reminder that Jesus has power over that which we fear most: illness and death. Most of us suffer from some physical malady, and if we don't, we almost certainly will. What is more certain is that we all will die. It's natural to wonder what lies on the other side of the parted curtain.

Jesus' miracles when He was here on earth were wonderful, but they did not change the world. Everyone He healed eventually got sick and died. What changed the world—and our lives in the world—is His death and resurrection, which guarantee eternal life to all who believe on Him. At the tomb of Lazarus He said, "I am the resurrection and the life. He who believes in me will live, even though he dies; and whoever lives and believes in me will never die. Do you believe this?" (John 11:25-26).

Yes, many times there is no healing, and the young die far too soon. Our prayers go unanswered. Frequently we are not sure of God's purpose in tragic situations. But there is something of which we can be sure: pain and suffering are intended by God to get our attention that we might learn to trust even when we cannot understand. "We rejoice in our sufferings, knowing that suffering produces endurance, and endurance produces character, and character produces hope, and hope does not put us to shame, because God's love has been poured into our hearts through the Holy Spirit who has been given to us" (Romans 5:3-5, ESV).

Through our suffering, Jesus stands triumphant over disease and death and invites us to participate in His victory. "I am the Living One; I was dead, and behold I am alive for ever and ever! And I hold the keys of death and Hades" (Revelation 1:18).

A PRAYER

Father, help me to realize that You care about me as a person, someone with a name and a specific need. Thank You for the assurance that You are trustworthy, able to keep the promises in Your Word. Give me the faith to believe in Your loving presence even when I experience physical pain and emotional distress. Give me the faith of the woman who touched You and was healed. In Jesus' name, Amen.

The teachers of the law and the Pharisees brought in a woman caught in adultery. They made her stand before the group and said to Jesus, "Teacher, this woman was caught in the act of adultery. In the Law Moses commanded us to stone such women. Now what do you say?" They were using this question as a trap, in order to have a basis for accusing him.

But Jesus bent down and started to write on the ground with his finger. When they kept on questioning him, he straightened up and said to them, "If any one of you is without sin, let him be the first to throw a stone at her." Again he stooped down and wrote on the ground.

At this, those who heard began to go away one at a time, the older ones first, until only Jesus was left, with the woman still standing there. Jesus straightened up and asked her, "Woman, where are they? Has no one condemned you?"

"No one, sir," she said.

"Then neither do I condemn you," Jesus declared. "Go now and leave your life of sin." JOHN 8:3-11

6

JESUS, LOVER OF AN ADULTEROUS WOMAN

Shari, a close friend of ours, grew up in a "Christian" home with a father who was often angry, harsh, controlling, and abusive. She married in her late teens to escape the home environment. But her husband turned out to be dishonest and unfaithful. When that marriage ended, Shari went through some extensive, excruciating trials, but through it all her faith in God's love and care was unshakable. Her love for Jesus was obvious as she openly shared her faith with others. She longed to find a man who was gentle, kind, patient, and visibly lived his faith. But because she was a people pleaser, Shari was sometimes unable to judge a person's true character.

As the years passed, Shari settled in a small, southwestern town. She worked with an itinerant country preacher. She was drawn to his enthusiastic personality, knowledge of Scripture, and ability to quote well-known authors. He, in turn, was drawn to her joyful countenance and her desire to discuss Bible doctrine. They spent time together and enjoyed talking about various Scripture passages and the issues of life. Shari began to pray about their relationship. He was just the type of man that appealed to her—kind, thoughtful, attentive, and spiritually minded. Was this bachelor the man for her?

Subtly, the preacher began to make comments that were, at

best, slightly inappropriate. When she felt uncomfortable and questioned him, he would give his comments a spiritual twist. How could she doubt his sincerity, godliness, and convincing words? Finally, he asked her to prove her love and devotion by sleeping with him. Shari knew this was wrong, but she was confused. So many things seemed right about this man, and by now he had won her heart. He continued to persuasively pressure her, and in the end she succumbed to the power of their physical attraction.

Immediately, Shari knew that what they had done was sinful; she knew she had grieved her Lord, and that the relationship with this man must end. Days later, she discovered that she was one of several women this man had courted in the same manner and with the same consequences. She felt guilty, dirty, and humiliated. She sought counsel from another pastor, forgiveness from God, and restoration with friends and family.

Like the woman who was brought to Jesus, Shari learned a painful lesson about deception, God's forgiveness, and what it means to "go and sin no more."

৩৫

A woman who has committed adultery is a woman who has betrayed her heart. The woman in John 8 had given power to a man who had probably used and manipulated her. And now the secret was exposed for all to see. In the presence of her accusers, she burned with shame.

We can put the pieces of her story together. It is one that has been told a thousand times. Her husband might have been abusive and cruel. In those days a woman was regarded as a man's property, so she could be divorced for just burning the toast! She endured his beatings and unkindness because she was trapped.

Lonely. Unloved. Her heart betrayed her into thinking that

she could find love and safety in another man's arms. But such an act was forbidden by the Mosaic law, and the penalty was more frightening than an occasional beating. Adultery was to be punished by stoning.

Against her protests, she found herself being dragged into the temple area, her face flushed with embarrassment. These men were bent on using her to entrap Jesus so they could accuse Him of sin. They were willing to exploit this woman's disgrace for their own evil purposes. They hated Jesus and hoped to bring Him to ruin.

Jesus' message and miracles created many followers who thought He might be either a prophet or the Messiah. His teachings conflicted with the traditions of the scribes and Pharisees, and the claims He made for Himself confounded the wisest among them. This carpenter's son's expertise in the Scriptures irked the religious leaders, who were taken aback by His breathtaking authority. They envied His following, so they frequently came to Him with trick questions or situations designed to entrap Him. They would have liked nothing better than to see Him arrested and killed.

They knew that Jesus could be found in the temple area, so that is where the men brought the accused woman. Jesus was sitting, teaching in the courtyard, when suddenly His attention was distracted. "The teachers of the law and the Pharisees brought in a woman caught in adultery. They made her stand before the group and said to Jesus, 'Teacher, this woman was caught in the act of adultery. In the Law Moses commanded us to stone such women. Now what do you say?' They were using this question as a trap, in order to have a basis for accusing him" (John 8:3-6).

At this point, we must say that this story is not in some of the earliest manuscripts of the New Testament; whether it should have been included in John's Gospel is a matter of debate. But almost all scholars admit that the story fits well into the context of the narrative and is consistent with the actions and teaching of Jesus. In other words, we can be assured this incident happened, whether it was in the original manuscripts or not.

Augustine says that certain individuals had removed this account from their manuscripts for fear that women would appeal to it as an excuse for their infidelity. The fear was that they would take the words, "Neither do I condemn you," as a license to sin. But grace always runs the risk of being misused. This is a story of hope for sinners, not an excuse to be flippant about our transgressions.

As we examine this drama, consider the startling difference between Jesus and the woman's eager accusers. He sends the woman away forgiven and her accusers are the ones who slink away in shame. Brilliant. A compassionate but clever turn of events.

THE MEN WHO ACCUSED HER

The Pharisees, who were experts in interpreting the law of Moses, caused this disturbance, hoping to create a dilemma for Jesus. Dragging this woman into the Temple before Him while He was teaching would mean a public humiliation both for the woman and for Jesus. It was the perfect opportunity to discredit Him before His followers.

Possibly these men belonged to the Sanhedrin and it was their intention to take her before that body to be sentenced. Her arrest may have been ordered by the temple police. One thing is certain: they brought her before Jesus in an attempt to mock Him. If He had the authority to judge as He claimed, then this was His case. This was an "in-your-face" confrontation.

Consider the quandary: Jesus had to either show disrespect for the law of Moses (which would be the case if He were to say "don't stone her") or He had to disregard the Roman law, which mandated that the Jews did not have the authority to put anyone to death. Also, if Jesus were to insist that she be stoned, He would lose His reputation as a man of mercy and compassion.

So Jesus was placed on the horns of a dilemma. Either He would be an enemy of God's law or an enemy of the Roman law, open to condemnation in either case. Indeed, this was a trick question intended to make Him look foolish. For we read, "They were using this question as a trap, in order to have a basis for accusing him" (v. 6).

They probably hoped that He would command them *not* to stone her, in which case He could be branded as transgressing the law of Moses. Keep in mind that they were not interested in what happened to this woman; they were interested only in finding a cause to bring a charge against Jesus. He, not the woman, was their intended victim.

The idea that the law should be combined with an attitude of restoration and compassion never entered their minds. They wanted to make sure that every lawbreaker paid every last cent for his or her transgression. Their attitude was one of unforgiving punishment. They were planning to murder Jesus, and as such were guilty of something far worse than the charge of adultery leveled against this hapless woman. But hardened hearts are not interested in the truth, only in proclaiming their own version of it.

Let's not forget that the worst sinners are often the greatest accusers.

This pious group prided itself in its righteousness, but it was a hideous kind of righteousness. Human nature being what it is, the more base or corrupt a man is, the more likely he will sit in judgment of others. The more untruthful he is, the more he will suspect others of lying; the more immoral he is, the more likely he will suspect others of immorality. Think of all those who hide their own wickedness under a zealous passion to condemn others.

Many a woman has been abused by men who were the best at praying long prayers and quoting Scripture. In contrast, those who are most aware of their own sinfulness are the most reluctant to judge or misuse others. Yes, they do judge when necessary, but they do so with a heavy heart and with a spirit of introspection, asking, "Is it I?" They know that they are just as capable of doing what others have done.

THE WOMAN AND SHAME

The disgrace and fear brought to this woman by her public display meant nothing to these men. She may have even been forced to appear unclothed. She was regarded as a *thing* to be used for their purposes; she was a pawn in their plan to destroy Jesus. As she cowered in the presence of these gawkers, unable to look into their evil eyes, she felt the humiliation of this mock trial. There was no mercy to be found.

If she felt anger, it was justified. Where was the man? Since they claimed this woman was caught in the very *act* of adultery, they would have known who the man was. If the authorities had really been intent on following the law of Moses, they would have brought the woman *and the man* to Jesus for stoning.

So this woman deeply felt the injustice of it all as she faced her accusers alone in disgrace and embarrassment. Perhaps, somehow, she realized that the real reason she was there was because they were bent on destroying Jesus.

JESUS' RESPONSE

With every eye and ear tuned in His direction, Jesus surprised those around Him by refusing to give a quick answer. "But Jesus bent down and started to write on the ground with his finger.

Various explanations have been given as to what Jesus might have written. Some say He wrote the names of the men who had brought this woman to Him. Or it is suggested that He wrote a word of warning that was aimed at the woman's accusers. One writer says that Jesus simply doodled because He was not interested in such questions since He had not come to judge but to save.

William Barclay offers a slightly different possibility. "It might well be that the leering, lustful look on the faces of the Scribes and Pharisees, the bleak cruelty in their eyes, the prurient curiosity of the crowd, the shame of the woman, all combined to twist the very heart of Jesus in agony and pity, so that He hid His eyes."[1] We are struck by the contrast between these men and Jesus. They were full of unholy excitement, passionate about their accusation, anxious to catch Him in a trap. Jesus, on the other hand, was calm and composed and full of compassion rather than condemnation.

Although we don't know what Jesus wrote, it is safe to say that this act added drama to the event. Since He took His time to answer, it is clear that everyone around Him waited breathlessly for what He would say. It also gave Jesus an opportunity to convey to this self-righteous group what they needed to know: their guilt was greater than hers.

OUT OF STONES TO THROW

The atmosphere was tense and awkward. The men grew impatient, agitated, as they continued to question Him. We can imagine them asking, "Well, what do you say . . . do you stand with Moses on this? Or do you agree with the Roman law?" They thought they had Him backed into a corner—there was no way that He could get out of this one. And if He gave no answer at all, He could be branded a coward. But Jesus wasn't quick to give an answer. "There is often a power in holy silence that no words, however eloquent, can carry."[2]

Finally, Jesus rose to His feet to speak. His piercing gaze looked right into their hearts. "Let him who is without sin among you throw the first stone at her." Ingeniously, He did not set aside the law of Moses . . . indeed, *He commanded them to stone her.* The only requirement was that the man who would throw the first stone had to be someone who was not guilty of the *same sin*, either in act or in thought. It was a brilliant answer! It was the kind of answer only Jesus could give.

By saying this, Jesus invoked a law that allowed those who brought an accusation that required the death penalty to throw the stones (Deuteronomy 17:7). And, by implication, the only person who has a right to pass judgment is someone who himself is not guilty of the same sin. These men were ensnared in the very trap they had set for Jesus.

As the words of Jesus hit their intended target, He once again bent down and wrote on the ground. These men, blinded by their own self-righteousness, had a momentary awakening of the conscience. "At this, those who heard began to go away one at a time, the older ones first, until only Jesus was left, with the woman still standing there" (v. 9). When Jesus required that those who would stone this woman should themselves be innocent, every man had a flashback of his own immorality.

The younger men, seeing the older ones walking away with bowed heads, chose to follow them, finding themselves unable to pick up the stones they had so eagerly gathered. We can visualize them as they quietly left, one by one, from the oldest to the youngest, until all of them were gone. This story is usually called, "Jesus and the Adulterous Woman," but actually it could be titled, "Jesus and the Adulterous Men."

They left because they had been outdone. They did not get a response from Jesus that they could use to denounce Him. They became aware, however briefly, of their own sinfulness. Conscience-smitten, they could not stand in the presence of this woman and in the presence of Jesus who knew them only too well. If they had repented of the hypocrisy that was uncovered in their own hearts, this could have been their moment of salvation.

But their hearts were as hard as the stones they were so ready to throw.

JESUS AND THE WOMAN

The crowd had stayed in the outer perimeter as these events were unfolding. The Greek text says that after the men left, the woman was standing before Jesus "in the midst," which would mean that others who had been drawn into this drama waited to see it to the end. Many no doubt overheard the subsequent conversation between Jesus and the woman.

> Jesus straightened up and asked her, "Woman,
> where are they? Has no one condemned you?"
> "No one, sir," she said.

Of course, Jesus knew that her accusers had been silenced. But He wanted her to affirm that, indeed, she was no longer being condemned by the religious leaders who had the right and power to stone her. He wanted her to know that she need not fear them. He also wanted her to know that He was in the position to grant her the forgiveness she desperately needed.

> "Then neither do I condemn you." Jesus
> declared. "Go now and leave your life of sin."
> (John 8:10-11)

These are the sweetest words that this woman had ever heard. Not just any man, but Jesus, the Lord, had lifted the condemnation from her heart. He did not deem her unfit for the Kingdom, if she repented. To Him, she was not just a thing, but a human being who mattered. She mattered in this life, and most assuredly she mattered in the life to come. As for her accusers, "They knew the thrill of exercising the power to condemn; Jesus knew the thrill of exercising the power to forgive."[3] This woman knew she was in the presence of One who had the authority to speak those words of forgiveness and cleansing.

Jesus did not approve of her conduct; He understood the severity of her sin. Morally, she was to be condemned, but judicially, He set her free. Her conscience was cleansed and her relationship with God was established. "He did not come to stone bodies to death, but to save souls to life."[4]

His words, "Go now and leave your life of sin" mean that her past was behind her, and she was expected to live differently in the future. "Let bygones be bygones; let oblivion cover thy past; let virtue crown thy future."[5] She left the temple area with the light of heaven on her face. Jesus knew that gracious forgiveness motivates us to a life of goodness.

THE GOD OF THE SECOND CHANCE

This woman's story, like ours, was unfinished. We do not know how she lived the rest of her days, but what we do know is that she experienced the gift of the second chance.

Jesus could grant her forgiveness because He was on His way to the cross; soon He would die for sinners, this woman included. There, her shame, like ours, would be taken away. "Let us fix our eyes on Jesus, the author and perfecter of our faith, who for the joy set before him endured the cross, *scorning its shame*, and sat down at the right hand of the throne of God" (Hebrews 12:2, emphasis added). Jesus endured shame so that we can be free from its stain and power. No one has to be bound by a past that has been forgiven by the Lawmaker and Judge of the universe.

Many a woman, humiliated and shamed, has discovered that Christ alone stands by her. Friends walk out. A lover abandons her.

Desolate.

Branded.

Forsaken.

The accusers carry their whispers into the church. But in the presence of Jesus she finds a listening ear, a compassionate heart, and forgiveness.

Jesus doesn't listen to our accusers. He already knows our sin and waits for us to come into His presence voluntarily. In love and compassion He speaks the same words He did so long ago, "Neither do I condemn you." No sin is too great to be forgiven. With the same authority He sets us free to begin again by saying, "Go now and leave your life of sin." No one else can give us that kind of help and hope.

FOR THIS

I've been looking for a fire
*   to burn my sin away.*
I've been looking for a flood
*   to cleanse my vilest ways.*
I've been looking for a knife
*   to cut out my iniquity.*
I've been looking for a death to die
*   to set my spirit free.*
My shame is not my glory
*   instead it is my noose.*
Held tightly by the reigns of sin
*   it will not let me loose.*
But now I see my search as vain

and in sheer futility,
For I've been looking to remove
what's stained the whole of me.
What hope have I of future love—
knowing what I know?
The stench of my sin is vast and foul;
I deserve the lowest of the low.
Yet even as I ponder,
I am adding to my shame,
For have I not found the fire, the flood,
the knife—is it not plain?
Have I forgotten the price 'twas paid
to remove the debt I owe?
Could it be that I've ignored
the grace that I've been shown?
For on the cross my sin was burned,
my transgression washed asea.
My wicked heart was carved anew—
a death to set me free!
Sorrow no more, oh heart of guilt—
your Savior has redeemed.
Your sin has been removed and cleansed,
washed under Calvary's stream.
Hope in God for He has bought
what you could never buy.
You've been forgiven, changed, renewed!
For this the Savior died.

Anonymous

All who have been involved in sexual sin can find forgiveness and cleansing in the presence of Jesus. To all He says, "Go and sin no more."

Who will bring any charge against those whom
God has chosen? It is God who justifies. Who is
he that condemns? Christ Jesus, who died—
more than that, who was raised to life—is at the
right hand of God and is also interceding for us.
(Romans 8:33-34)

A PRAYER

*Heavenly Father, I receive Your forgiveness and cleansing for
those sins that I know about, as well as those I'm not aware
of. I know that I cannot manage them or wish them away. I
ask that You remove my guilt and restore my purity and
wholeness.*

*Lord, help me to extend Your grace to the helpless; let
me reach out to those who think they are unreachable, to
show kindness to those who bear the shame of a sordid past.
Bring into my life those who need the forgiveness that You
extend to all who come before You in humility and honesty.
May all who are Your children hear You say, "Neither do I
condemn you; go and sin no more." In Jesus' name, Amen.*

As Jesus and his disciples were on their way, he came to a village where a woman named Martha opened her home to him. She had a sister called Mary, who sat at the Lord's feet listening to what he said. But Martha was distracted by all the preparations that had to be made. She came to him and asked, "Lord, don't you care that my sister has left me to do the work by myself? Tell her to help me!"

"Martha, Martha," the Lord answered, "you are worried and upset about many things, but only one thing is needed. Mary has chosen what is better, and it will not be taken away from her."   LUKE 10: 38-42

7

JESUS, LOVER OF THE WORRIED AND ANXIOUS

The story of Mary and Martha has always fascinated me (Rebecca). It has also troubled me. How could Jesus scold Martha for working hard and doing what was necessary, while He commended Mary for being lazy? Many years passed before I understood the true meaning of what Jesus was teaching. I must tell you my story and why I have struggled with this narrative in the life of Jesus.

When I was eleven years old, my family of eight moved into a partially finished structure a half mile off the highway by dirt road. There was no flushing toilet, no telephone, no TV. The only furniture was a kitchen table and chairs and our beds. The only appliances were a refrigerator, stove (the lone source of heat), and a washing machine. When it rained, the roof leaked in several places. This thirty-by-thirty foot shack had just one dividing wall. Boxes of clothes, books, and junk created small spaces that became our "rooms." Prior to this move, we had lived in a variety of locations, enduring hardship and poverty and tremendous family conflict.

My father and mother endured a stormy, destructive marriage. They met and married during World War II (both were in the military). Vastly different backgrounds and painful memories of the Depression left them ill prepared for the challenges of marriage and parenthood. Anger and regret fueled heated arguments. In the mid-to-late forties, my father worked part-time and attended a seminary program, hoping to go into full-time ministry. But marital conflict and my mother's health problems prevented this. She was emotionally and physically unable to take care of six children and the household.

Trying to cope with these difficult circumstances, my parents severely disciplined us for both real and imagined disobedience. Cruel words and actions wounded our spirits and bodies. I often wondered why I had been born into this family. Poverty, neglect, and abuse produced shame and humiliation in all of us. At school, I felt so different from my classmates. But my one redeeming quality was that I was smart and could help those who struggled with homework and study questions.

As the oldest daughter (second born), it was my responsibility to cook and wash the dishes. There were also endless loads of laundry to wash, hang out to dry, and later fold. Sometimes I even had to care for livestock. My younger siblings needed attention, instruction, and care. There was no time for studying as I fell into bed exhausted each night. Schoolwork had to wait until the early morning hours, when my father woke me to iron his shirt before he left for work. And then, I was sometimes fortunate enough to get an uninterrupted hour in which I could study and do homework before walking a mile and a half to school. Occasionally, I made it to the highway in time to ride the school bus.

Strangely, in this harsh atmosphere, my parents did love God and taught us to revere and love the Bible. Sometimes, we were required to sit quietly and listen to various radio Bible teachers. At Christmastime, we always listened to the entire *Messiah* on an old reel-to-reel tape recorder. Our family attended a small Bible church, and in the summers I loved going to a Christian camp in another state. But no one could have imagined what was going on inside our home. It was a sad, dark, painful secret.

In spite of all of this, I grew up with a desire and longing to know God. I accepted Christ as my Savior at the age of seven and wanted to be a missionary nurse. Somehow I knew that life should be different from what mine was. In my teen years, I sometimes slipped from my cot at night and read my Bible by the pilot light of the water heater. I was sustained by believing that God really did love me. I always had the hope that there was something better out there, and that I must survive in order to find it. I actually believed that God had a plan for my life.

It was from this environment that I left to attend Bible college in the mid-sixties, hoping to fulfill my long-term dream of becoming a missionary nurse. But God had a different plan for me, and three months after graduating in 1969, I married a promising young professor/preacher. When it became apparent that I would become a pastor's wife, I thought God had made a mistake—this was the one thing I had told God I never wanted to be. More than you can ever imagine, I was unprepared for this role. I had never seen my mother entertain or practice hospitality. She had no dining or living room furniture. No china, silverware, lovely furnishings, or nice pictures on the wall. How would I know what to do as a pastor's wife?

God was asking me to do the impossible. I was shy, scared, and felt inferior to the women in our first church. No one knew of my background. But God was challenging me to overcome these obstacles and learn how to be hospitable and show mercy and kindness to others. When we were invited to someone's home for dinner, I would take mental notes on how to set the table, what to serve, and how to serve it. I was awed by the beautiful homes and furnishings of our parishioners. I once told my husband that if I had a thousand dollars, I wouldn't even know what to buy to make our home look lovely.

As time passed, however, I began to gain confidence. But just like Martha, I was worried and anxious about preparing for and serving my guests. With small children to care for and a busy husband, I had no one to help me. I fretted and often felt under enormous stress. What would people think about my home and my presentation? How could I possibly serve them with the same grace and ability with which they had served us? I knew that it really didn't matter what they thought, as my ministry of hospitality should be done for the Lord, but I was still nervous and apprehensive.

Over the years, as I have practiced and honed my skills, I've come to realize that the state of my heart is far more important than the state of my home, though there is correlation between the two and one affects the other. I have had to learn how to set aside my Martha-like tendencies and become more like Mary—to worship and sit at Jesus' feet first. And in doing so, God has taught me how to open my home to others in confidence and joy rather than worry and apprehension.

໖໐

Who is the woman in the New Testament with whom most high-powered, performance-oriented women identify? You've answered correctly if you said *Martha*. Many women wear their identification with Martha as a badge of courage; they pride themselves in getting things done.[1] It must be just a coincidence that Martha Stewart is so named! If all women were like Mary, spending time at the feet of Jesus, who would make the meals and clean the house? Who would take the kids to school, keep a husband happy, and hold down a part-time job on the side? It is the Marthas who make the world turn round, not the mystical Marys.

But Mary found the freedom to do what women in her day never did: sit at the feet of a rabbi in a public setting. Incredibly, Jesus, contrary to expectations, never questioned her competence to hear His Word. The relaxed atmosphere that Jesus fostered was simply not the norm. In the culture of the day, both Jesus and Mary would have been censured for an improper relationship—Jesus for talking so freely to a woman at close range and in public, and Mary for having the audacity to think that her behavior was proper, that she really mattered to Jesus, and that He appreciated her focused attention.

Author Don Hawkins reports that when he speaks about Martha, women frequently come to him and say, "I'm so much like Martha!" But virtually no woman says, "I'm so much like Mary!" In fact, the impression is that the Marys of this world are lazy and have messy houses. Therefore, Martha seems to have a corner on the feminine market.[2] Clearly something in this story seems to be amiss if we think that it justifies a lackadaisical approach to living. Or that it is critical of women who are diligent, hard-working, ambitious, and want to join the competitive workforce.

In fact, in the Christian community, homemaking—caring for children, decorating, cooking, and being hospitable—is high on the list of things to be honored. Christian women often feel their worth is measured by this standard.

Since Jesus gives Mary high praise and rebukes Martha for her anxious activity, we had better take a second look at this story and ask, how can we have the approval of Jesus as Mary did and still perform like Martha? We shall discover that we do not have to make a choice between being a worker like Martha and a worshipper like Mary.

Jesus frequently enjoyed the company of three friends who

lived in Bethany, which was located on the eastern slope of the Mount of Olives, about two miles from Jerusalem. Sisters Martha and Mary, with their brother Lazarus, were the nearest thing to a family circle that Jesus experienced. "Their home in Bethany was one of the few places where He could be away from curious stares and constant demands."[3] Here were ordinary folk who accepted Him, served Him, and expected few favors in return. Even Jesus needed to draw the strength that comes from those who knew Him the best and accepted Him without great expectations.

We'd like to know where Jesus met these two women and their brother. Were they among the throngs that gathered when He was in Jerusalem? Did Jesus just stop by and ask for a cup of water or a place to rest? We'll never know. Though the text does not say so, we can surmise that the twelve disciples were also with Jesus, since they accompanied Him on His journeys. So Martha had her hands full as she scrambled to feed about fifteen or sixteen people that day.

As we read the story, focus on the different ways these two sisters welcomed their honored guest. Martha, evidently the eldest, ran the household and kept things in order. She appeared to be an active and practical person, whereas Mary would likely have preferred writing poems to washing pans.[4] We commend these sisters for opening their home to Jesus when others, perhaps, were uneasy and even afraid to host Him.

Lazarus is not mentioned in this story, but he figures prominently in the dramatic account of his sickness, death, and resurrection. There we read, "Jesus loved Martha and her sister and Lazarus" (John 11:5). Later, Jesus wept at the tomb of Lazarus as He sought to comfort the grieving sisters. It appears that Martha and Mary depended on Jesus as sisters might depend upon an elder brother.

There are two other references to this family in Scripture, both occurring in the Gospel of John. In all three unforgettable scenes, the sisters display the same characteristics. One is the busy, efficient woman and the other is found at Jesus' feet.

This is a familiar contrast of temperaments. Martha was the controlling personality, the one who was in charge of the home. That is likely why Luke records, "Martha welcomed him into *her* house" (Luke 10:38, ESV, emphasis added). She probably was not the exclusive owner, but she was its exclusive boss. Mary represents those whose personality is more noticeable for who they are than for what they do.

It's probably easy to identify more with Martha than with Mary because we all have a tendency to vie for control, convincing ourselves that we have the best of motives. We want things to be done right, and there is only one way to insure that that will happen: do it ourselves or tell others how it should be done. Martha certainly seems to be the dominant, more common personality.

I (Rebecca) understand how women feel, and how easy it is to get caught in this trap. Being the oldest daughter in my family, I had the responsibility to work hard and make decisions for the good of everyone. Certainly, it was easier to do the work myself than to teach younger siblings how to do it. I carried this habit into our marriage and often felt compelled to do the work myself or to tell my husband and daughters how to do it the "right" way. I've had to learn to back off and acknowledge that there is more than one right way to do something. We are either born with this kind of personality or learn this attitude through our circumstances. Whichever it was for Martha, she had a difficult time getting Mary to cooperate.

There is another issue here that seems unfair. Both in the home and in the church, women are often relegated to the kitchen while the men discuss "the important things." Obviously, the majority of women are more competent in the kitchen than are men, but women also have intelligent minds and hungry hearts that long to discuss theology and learn from Scripture. No doubt, it's time to ask the men to join *us* in the kitchen to get the preparations and cleanup completed in less time, so that we can join *them* for theological discussion and fellowship. Martha probably wanted Mary's help so that she might have time to join her sister at the feet of Jesus.

We cannot read this story without recognizing the contrast between these two women. Jesus, as we shall learn, did not expect Martha to become Mary, nor Mary to become Martha. But He did help Martha understand something about her attitude and priorities. Let's see how each is portrayed in this beautiful story.

Consider the contrasts.

SERVING VERSUS SITTING

We can visualize the scene in our minds.

"She had a sister called Mary, who sat at the Lord's feet listening to what he said" (Luke 10:39). Middle Eastern homes usually had a large couch that was raised about two feet from the floor along the wall; often these sofas doubled as beds. Jesus was sitting there, perhaps with His legs crossed, speaking and answering questions. Mary is sitting at His feet, on a rug or mat, hanging on to every word. This for her was a cherished moment to connect with this loving man whom she was coming to know as the Son of God. "By her attentive hearing Mary helped to make the seat of Jesus a pulpit, her own humble place at his feet a pew, and the whole room a chapel in which the mercy of Jehovah was proclaimed, yea a very sanctuary where God himself drew nigh to the sinful heart with grace."[5]

There was a magnetism to the words of Jesus that Mary

found irresistible. He didn't have to shout; His whispers were even more intriguing than His public pronouncements. She listened as a lily opens itself to the sun. She picked up on the mood of Jesus and knew that He would prefer this fellowship to an elaborate spread of food. For this visit, a simple meal was to be preferred, rather than enjoying the best the sisters could give. This was a time when worship was more important than work, and sitting was more important than serving.

Martha—bless her—was overburdened with the serving; she was making appropriate, if not elaborate, preparations for the meal that was about to begin. She also loved their honored guest. But she needed help, and she resented her younger sister who sat there enjoying fellowship with Jesus, unaware of the controlling realities of the moment. She was vexed within herself, for there were tasks that still needed to be done.

Keep in mind that Martha loved Jesus too. She loved Him deeply and would have very much liked to sit beside her sister and listen to His gracious words. But in her mind, first things should come first; there was a meal to be prepared and refreshments to be served. Let these matters be taken care of first, and time with Jesus would follow.

Mary appeared oblivious to her sister's tense demeanor. Every time Martha walked by, she hoped that her sister would catch a hint that she should join her in the preparations. When Mary did not pick up on the hints, Martha became irritated and peevishly asked, "Lord, don't you care that my sister has left me to do the work by myself? Tell her to help me!" (v. 40).

She was not being disrespectful; after all, she did call Jesus "Lord." She was just pointing out the obvious: she was serving alone and it would not be unreasonable for her sister to "take hold at her end" as the Greek text implies. She wanted Mary to carry her part of the load. The work of the household should be shared, as should the fellowship with Jesus. So she blamed Jesus for letting Mary get by without helping. She did not speak to her sister directly, knowing that Mary just might ignore her wishes. But Martha knew that if Jesus asked Mary to help, she'd jump at His command.

However reasonable the request seems, we should be startled. Here is Martha giving advice to Jesus, the Lord, the Omnipotent One! And yet this is not the only time Martha tries to correct Jesus. At the tomb of Lazarus, Jesus says, "Take away the stone" and Martha objects, "Lord, by this time there is a bad odor, for he has been there four days" (John 11:39). She feels the need to explain to the Lord the process of decomposition. Yet she represents all of us who become demanding in our prayers, often explaining to God why He *should* answer, and how we expect the answer to come. She is neither the first nor the last person to believe that Jesus needed additional information.

Martha was task oriented. She knew what had to be done and set out to do it to the best of her ability. She was purpose driven, that is, driven by the need to provide the food that the occasion demanded. As we shall see, this was not wrong in itself, but as one person put it, such personalities run the risk of becoming a "human doing" rather than a human being.[6] She just might have been the type of person who says, "I am having a nervous breakdown . . . don't talk me out of it; I deserve it."

But Martha was surprised by Jesus' response. She expected Him to agree with her. Instead of rebuking Mary, or at least suggesting that she help her sister, Jesus directed His words back to Martha instead. He did not chide Martha for serving, but for allowing her mind to be distracted from something that was more important. Her attentiveness to serving had gotten the best of her. To Martha's surprise, Jesus pointed out that Mary had better priorities than she (Martha) did.

Sometimes it is better to sit than to serve. When we really understand the principle that Jesus is teaching here, we can confess our anxiety, anger, and annoyance. Our communion with God is the "one thing that is needful." Nothing can give satisfaction to our lives except being in union with the divine. "Many things we may have, but one thing we must have; many things are useful; others are important, but only one thing is really necessary."[7]

MANY THINGS VERSUS THE ONE THING

Jesus knew that Martha had taken on too much. But He did not ask Mary to jump to her feet to help her troubled sister. Rather, He said, "Martha, Martha, you are worried and upset about many things, but only one thing is needed. Mary has chosen what is better, and it will not be taken away from her" (vv. 41-42). He called her name twice, the double reference being a mark of special love. Jesus gently reached out towards Martha's heart. He pointed out that her mind was distracted, divided between her domestic responsibilities and the special opportunity that her sister had chosen.

The Greek word for *worried* or *anxious* means to distract or divide. Martha was overwhelmed by all of her responsibilities; she was, for the moment, a woman with competing and divided interests. Jesus used the same word *worried* five times in Matthew 6:19-34 to point out the dangers of anxiety. "So do not worry, saying, 'What shall we eat?' or 'What shall we drink?' or 'What shall we wear?' For the pagans run after all these things, and your heavenly Father knows that you need them. But seek first his kingdom and his righteousness, and all these things will be given to you as well" (Matthew 6:31-33). Martha was so focused on her work that she forgot there were other matters that were more important.

She was too concerned about many things that were not absolutely necessary for the occasion. The table arrangements and the extra decorations had consumed too much of her time and energy. Jesus is not saying that food and preparation are unnecessary; He is saying that the trivia of life should not take over.[8] It was not what Martha was doing that was wrong; it was what she was *neglecting* that concerned Jesus. Her priorities were out of line with the opportunity that was before her. Might it be—and we only suggest it—that Martha's overzealous hospitality was not so much for the benefit of Jesus as it was for her own benefit in the compliments she would later receive?

To hear the voice of Jesus with an open heart is better than any work, sacrifice, or even suffering. To close our ears to Jesus for any reason at all—no matter how pressing or significant—is to close ourselves off from the fellowship for which Jesus longs. "Too many of us show the Martha-like traits of fussiness, fault-finding, tantrums and anxiety. Too often, these are dead giveaways that we have tried to make work a substitute for God. Being busy is not an excuse for not trusting and serving Him."[9]

In her eagerness to *serve* Jesus, Martha almost missed the opportunity to *know* Jesus.[10] Perhaps Mary had already helped prepare the meal, but she knew that the most important part of the evening was the time spent with Jesus.

Those who have changed their world have always had a single focus; they were not distracted by other worthwhile endeavors. As the apostle Paul says, "This one thing I do. . . ." Dwight L. Moody, a great evangelist of the nineteenth century was fond of saying, "This one thing I do. . . . not these forty things I dabble in." We cannot overestimate the power of even an average mind that is bent on one grand purpose.

A seventeenth-century writer, Henry Scougal, said that our soul cannot know what solid joy and pleasure is, "till once, being weary of itself, it renounces all propriety, and gives itself up unto the Author of its being . . . and can say, from an inward sense of feeling, 'My beloved is mine.'"[11] In fact, he says, if God were truly the object of our love, we should share our happiness without any possibility of its dwindling.

> *Jesus, thou joy of loving hearts*
> *Thou fount of life, thou light of men*
> *From the best bliss that earth imparts*
> *We turn unfilled, to thee again.*
>
> *Bernard of Clairvaux*

When we have enough of God to make us happy, we will discover that we have enough of God to change us, to help us get our priorities in the right order.

Martha learned that sometimes the good is the enemy of the best.

TEMPORARY VERSUS PERMANENT

Martha's conflicting priorities were no small matter.

Someone has said that two banquets were being served in that house: Martha was about to enjoy the physical food and Mary was enjoying the spiritual. The one thing that Mary began on earth is the one thing that will be continued in heaven. "While the world applauds achievement, God desires companionship. The world clamors, 'Do more! Be all that you can be!' But our Father whispers, 'Be still and know that I am God.'"[12]

In all the years to come, Mary surely cherished those precious moments at the feet of Jesus. She had looked into His loving face and connected with a fellowship that was more glorious than any meal could ever bring. Later, Jesus would give Himself for the sins of the world, and both Martha and Mary would benefit from this gracious provision. But—and this is important—Mary had received a glimpse of the eternal when Jesus visited, and perhaps, just perhaps, Martha missed that singular opportunity.

The cure for anxiety and a troubled mind are corrected by focusing on Jesus and His promises; by concentrating on the one needful thing. Martha, by being divided, was troubled and anxious. By being *un*divided in her focus, Mary found a rest for her soul.

Jesus would not allow Martha to draw Mary from the Word that He was speaking; He would not allow her to join Martha in having her attention divided among the many other things, no matter how kind or helpful.

Clearly, Jesus was inviting Martha to join her sister at His feet so both of them could accept "the good part." There will always be time to decorate, time to prepare, time to serve, time to eat. But Jesus was inviting Martha to enjoy the soul-satisfying fellowship He was there to offer on that day.

We picture both of them sitting at the feet of Jesus, delighting His heart by enjoying that which could never be taken from them. "Behold, I stand at the door and knock. If anyone hears my voice and opens the door, I will come in to him and eat with him, and he with me" (Revelation 3:20, ESV). The longing of Jesus was for closeness of mind and heart with those He loved. Martha had to be cleansed of the distractions that made it impossible for her to enjoy intimate fellowship.

But we are still left with the question: Does Jesus want all the Marthas of this world to become Marys? How do we achieve a balance between the contemplative and the active, the listeners and the talkers, the sitters and the servers? The answer lies in Jesus' words, "one thing is needful." Let's consider what that means.

FINDING THE BALANCE

Must we choose between being a Martha or a Mary? If we choose what is best, does that mean a woman—or a man, for that matter—cannot be industrious, creative, productive, and hospitable to others? Does "the good part" mean that we can only spend our lives in reading, contemplation, worship, and prayer?

No, of course not. Mary understood that this was a rare moment and chose to take advantage of it. Somehow, she comprehended that Jesus was on a trajectory, headed to the cross, that soon He would be with them no more. She wanted to spend every possible moment in His presence, listening to His words and worshipping at His feet. She evidently realized that this was not the moment to make Jesus a big meal; it would have been more appropriate to serve light refreshments on this occasion. In their enthusiasm and thoroughness, the Marthas of this world have a tendency to overprepare, overorganize, and overperform.

No doubt Martha learned her lesson well. Later, she prepared a feast for Jesus, the twelve disciples, other guests, and her brother and sister (that's close to twenty people), and she didn't complain, nor did Jesus chide her for wrong priorities. "Here a dinner was given in Jesus' honor. Martha served, while Lazarus was among those reclining at the table with Him" (see John 12:1-2). Here is proof that the Marthas of this world are indispensable to the family, and to life itself.

Yet, true to her nature, it is also here at this feast that Mary anoints the head and feet of Jesus and is rebuked by the disciples for her extravagance. It seems clear that Jesus would want us to imitate Mary in our worship, and Martha in our work. To expect Martha to become a Mary, or Mary to become a Martha, would deny the diversity of God's creation. Jesus is saying that few things are as damaging to the Christian life as attempting to do work for Him without taking time to fellowship and worship Him as well.

We often hear that we are to have the right priorities: Jesus first, our families and friends second, then our vocation, and ourselves last. This might seem like a solution, but in point of fact it is not. Our lives cannot be divided into these neat categories. What is more, it is unrealistic to think that we can spend as much time in Bible reading as we do working a forty- or fifty-hour workweek. These priorities seem right on paper, but they simply do not work out in practical experience.

We must allow our relationship with Jesus to extend over and above all of the other categories of responsibility. We work *in fellowship with Jesus*, we relate to our family responsibilities *in fellowship with Jesus,* and we take care of ourselves *in fellowship with Jesus.* Jesus is therefore always *first*—in our families, in our vocation, in our service at church. Properly understood, there can be no competition between our agenda and His. He must be Lord of all.

In her excellent book *Martha to the Max*, Debi Stack writes this about her struggle with what we could call the Martha syndrome: "For about twenty years now, since the peak of my workaholism, I've been sitting and listening. Somewhere along the way, I stopped being obsessed with defining '*one thing*' into a specific task to perform and evaluate. And I also learned this: sitting wasn't the *one thing*, but the *one thing* made Mary sit. Listening wasn't the *one thing* either but the *one thing* made Mary listen . . . perhaps *one thing* is not the thing to do, but a way to be; not a place to go, but a place to begin."[13]

The one thing is the communion of the soul with God through His Word; it is the enjoyment of eternal life, which begins now and never ends, even for all of eternity. And that can be the experience for everyone, no matter what personality, vocation, talent, or gift you have. We can all have a Mary heart in a Martha world.

A PRAYER

Heavenly Father, help me to be quiet in Your presence, to hear Your voice through Your Word and to take time to renew our friendship, just one on one. May the intimacy my soul craves be found through my submission to Your truth, and the faith to believe that You, O Father, and Your Son, Jesus, by your Spirit, have come to take up residence in my heart. Give me Mary's heart and Martha's diligence. In Jesus' name, Amen.

Six days before the Passover, Jesus arrived at Bethany, where Lazarus lived, whom Jesus had raised from the dead. Here a dinner was given in Jesus' honor. Martha served, while Lazarus was among those reclining at the table with him. Then Mary took about a pint of pure nard, an expensive perfume; she poured it on Jesus' feet and wiped his feet with her hair. And the house was filled with the fragrance of the perfume.

But one of his disciples, Judas Iscariot, who was later to betray him, objected, "Why wasn't this perfume sold and the money given to the poor? It was worth a year's wages." He did not say this because he cared about the poor but because he was a thief; as keeper of the money bag, he used to help himself to what was put into it.

"Leave her alone," Jesus replied. "It was intended that she should save this perfume for the day of my burial. You will always have the poor among you, but you will not always have me."   JOHN 12:1-8

JESUS, LOVER OF AN EXTRAVAGANT WOMAN

Many of you already know the story of Dorie Vanstone. She is well-known because of her two books, *Dorie, the Girl Nobody Loved* and *No Place to Cry*. She is, by all accounts, wildly in love with Jesus. Like Mary of Bethany, Dorie is generous, forgiving, and wholly devoted to her Lord. She spares nothing for His sake and for His glory.

Dorie came into our lives back in 1971 when we met her and her husband, Lloyd, at a conference. She had shared her childhood story with enthusiasm and grace, leaving us in tears—tears of grief that a child would have to suffer as she did, but also tears of gratitude that God could take someone who was born a nobody and make her into a somebody for His glory.

Dorie was conceived out of wedlock, born into a home where she was not wanted by either her mother or her father. When she was six years old, she was dropped off at an orphanage in Oakland, California. Her mother promised to visit, but came only twice in the next seven years. There, a member of the staff abused her physically and sexually—a story that has since been verified by others who were in the orphanage during the same period of time.

When a group of students from a local Bible college visited the orphanage, Dorie, ever the mean girl, was sitting on the floor intending to do mischief. The students finished their gospel presentation and were about to leave, when one turned and said, "Children, if you forget everything we've said, remember, *God loves you!*"

Dorie, with a bowed head, responded in her heart, *God, no one has ever loved me, but if you love me, you can have me.* That night, as always, she cried before going to sleep, but this time, it was with tears of joy. Something had happened within her, and she knew she had found God—or rather, God had found her.

After her time in the orphanage, Dorie was placed in a series of foster homes where she continued to be abused. But she connected with a church, was given a New Testament, and began to follow the Lord fully. She attended Bible college, married a godly man, and together they became missionaries among the headhunters of New Guinea.

Dorie's dear husband, Lloyd, died suddenly in 1985, and throughout all these lonely years, Dorie has traveled the United States and the world, sharing what God can do in giving hope to the abused, the neglected, and the unwanted of this world.

If Dorie had been present at the supper recorded in John 12, like Mary of Bethany, she would have been the first to break open her costly jar of perfume and anoint the feet of Jesus. Today, Dorie's life is characterized by extravagance. She supports missionaries with her meager income and she ministers tirelessly to the unwanted and rejected. "I was so desperate I threw myself at the Lord," she says. "And so the rest of my life is devoted to serving Him." With abandon she gives her life away for the One who accepted her when no one else would.

∞

Love is costly.

Just ask Mary of Bethany, who anointed Jesus with expensive

perfume. She redefined the meaning of the word *extravagant* and forever laid to rest the notion that love is cautious, calculating, and risk-free. With this one act of unabashed devotion, this woman changed her world.

Jesus, breaking with tradition, allowed a woman to touch and bless Him, and in return He predicted that her personal devotion to Him would be known by future generations. No wonder women were among His most devoted followers.

In contrast, the men of Jesus' day believed that women were intellectually inferior and incapable of spiritual and rational insights. Some rabbis even said that it was better that the words of the law should be burned than delivered to women.

But Jesus entrusted His Word to them. And they were not just a part of His ministry, but also among His closest friends and confidants.

The story of Jesus' anointing by Mary of Bethany occurs in three of the four Gospels—Matthew, Mark, and John. Although the details differ, it is clear that these writers are speaking about the same event. All of them place the incident in the final weeks as Jesus and His disciples were preparing for the Passover. Jesus, knowing He was soon going to die, spent some quiet time in the village of Bethany, in the home of Simon the leper, a man whom He had personally cured.

Here a dinner was given in Jesus' honor with the sisters Martha and Mary and their brother, Lazarus, present for the occasion. Martha served while Lazarus and others reclined at the table with Him. Then Mary quietly took about a pint of pure nard (an expensive perfume), poured it on Jesus' feet, and wiped His feet with her hair. Soon the house was filled with the fragrance of the perfume.

The disciples rebuked her for this extravagance, but once again Jesus came to the defense of a woman, pointing out that she had more spiritual insight than those who watched and criticized. This one act of devotion had great meaning to Him.

MARY OF BETHANY AND MARY MAGDALENE

Many recent books insist that the Mary who anointed Jesus on this special occasion must be Mary Magdalene. Some wish to use this incident as further proof that Jesus and Mary were intimate friends or lovers. In *The Woman with the Alabaster Jar*, Margaret Starbird points to traditions that link this Mary of Bethany with Mary Magdalene. In western art, for example, the woman depicted as carrying an alabaster jar is the penitent prostitute, who in those days was thought to be Mary Magdalene.

Contrary to these traditions, Mary of Bethany is not Mary Magdalene. She was always identified as the sister of Martha and of Lazarus. Mary Magdalene is always referred to as *Magdalene* because she was from Magdala near Galilee. She is consistently referred to as Mary Magdalene to keep her distinct from other women named Mary. We must acknowledge that there are three separate women: the prostitute of Luke 7; Mary Magdalene, who is introduced in Luke 8; and Mary of Bethany.

Understandably, this is confusing, as there are at least five different "Marys" that can be identified in the New Testament. Starbird admits, as indeed she must, that she cannot prove that Mary Magdalene was the woman who anointed Jesus at Bethany.[1] Only if we distinguish Mary of Bethany from Mary Magdalene can we accurately account for all the facts.

Mary of Bethany is named three times in the Gospels, and each time she is at the feet of Jesus (Luke 10:38-42; John 11:2, 31-32; 12:1-8). "Sitting at his feet" was an expression used in that day to refer to someone studying with a teacher. We've already learned how radical it was to let a woman take the place of a learner or a disciple.

THE FRAGRANCE THAT FILLED THE WORLD

For Jesus to come to Jerusalem for the Passover was an act of courage, since the authorities had made Him an outlaw (John 11:57). The divine clock was ticking. As each minute passed, He was brought ever closer to completing the plan of redemption. He would become the Passover Lamb for all of humanity. The victory predicted in Genesis 3:15, that Christ would be wounded by Satan, but that Satan would be crushed by Christ, would take place in a few days. The hosts of heaven and the evil spirits on earth were all waiting in anticipation of this cataclysmic event.

The purpose for which Jesus was born—to become the Savior of the world—was imminent. His mind and heart were heavy with the weight of the physical and spiritual suffering He knew was coming. In a few days He would say these words: "The hour has come for the Son of Man to be glorified. . . . Now my heart is troubled, and what shall I say? 'Father, save me from this hour'? No, it was for this very reason I came to this hour. Father, glorify your name!" (John 12:23, 27-28).

Jesus chose to spend the final days of His earthly life in Bethany. He is not recorded as doing a miracle there, but He gathered His closest friends and disciples around Him. Soon He would leave the protection of those who loved Him and step into the midst of an angry mob who hated Him. These were the matters that were on His mind.

On this night a dinner was given in His honor. As usual, Martha was cooking and serving, but this time she wasn't complaining. Her sister, Mary (of Bethany), who often sat at the feet of Jesus, listening to what He taught, was about to do something that would surprise everyone. Except Jesus. Her actions would reveal that she, unlike the disciples, understood the things Jesus had been teaching about Himself.

Jesus was reclining on a couch at a table. Mary came to him

with an alabaster jar, a small stone flask with a long, slender neck. It contained about a pint of perfume made of pure nard, an aromatic oil from a rare plant that is native to India. In keeping with ancient custom, she broke the neck of the flask, ensuring that it would never be used for anyone else again. She then poured the expensive perfume over Jesus' head and feet, and then wiped them with her hair. No respectable woman in that culture would have appeared in public with her hair unbound. But here, among friends and in the presence of Jesus, love became vulnerable. His feet needed to be wiped, and Mary threw custom to the wind.

The disciples' reaction showed how ignorant they were of Jesus' impending death. In Mark's account it is clear that the disciples joined Judas in rebuking her. He spoke for all of them, " 'Why wasn't this perfume sold and the money given to the poor? It was worth a year's wages.' He did not say this because he cared about the poor but because he was a thief; as keeper of the money bag, he used to help himself to what was put into it" (John 12:5-6).

Judas had a point. The cost of this pound of spikenard ointment was three hundred denarii, a year's wages. It was customary for a man to receive about a denarius a day for his work, but a woman would receive much less, if indeed she had a job at all. We must take a moment to imagine a year's worth of wages, contained in a little bottle. In fact, these kinds of jars with expensive perfume or jewelry were often kept in a home as a hedge against inflation. The perfume kept its value, despite the fluctuations of the currency at the time.

Judas represented a practical outlook that made sense to thinking people. Expensive perfume thrown away makes no sense to the person who has to scrounge for a decent living. Life is tough, and buying clothes and food can be a challenge even in the best of times.

Judas probably expected that Jesus would agree with him. Of course, his lofty talk about using the money for the poor hid a sinister motive. We read, "He did not say this because he cared about the poor but because he was a thief." He concealed his greed. He was also distressed to see someone love Jesus that deeply. As for himself, he was already plotting how he would go to the authorities to betray Jesus for thirty pieces of silver.

Jesus came to Mary's defense. "Leave her alone. . . . It was intended that she should save this perfume for the day of my burial. You will always have the poor among you, but you will not always have me" (John 12:7-8). In Mark, we have the added words, "I tell you the truth, wherever the gospel is preached throughout the world, what she has done will also be told, in memory of her" (14:9). What a promise to an unassuming woman from a humble home living in an insignificant town.

Amazing.

Here is a paraphrase: "Mary intentionally spent an enormous amount of money on an outrageously expensive perfume and saved it for this special occasion so that she could anoint Me on the eve of My death and burial." And He described her deed as a good or beautiful thing. Her love for Jesus motivated her, but in retrospect she was guided by a divine plan.

Mary could have simply told Jesus how much she loved Him, but talk is cheap. She wanted to *demonstrate* it. We can confidently say that she lavished her retirement account on Jesus. Her heart ran over with love. Love is reckless, never calculating the cost. The fragrance of this perfume has wafted down through the ages, and her story *has* been told in every generation, just as Jesus predicted. The fact that you are reading this is further proof.

Perhaps you remember the short story, "The Gift of the Magi." A young American couple, Della and Jim, were very poor but very much in love. Della's hair was her glory; when she let it down it was so long it almost served as her robe. Jim had a gold watch, which had come to him from his father and was his pride. The day before Christmas, they had nothing to give each other.

Della, deeply in love, decided to sell her hair for twenty dollars to buy her lover a platinum watch fob and chain for his beautiful watch. When Jim came home that night and saw Della, he paused, stupefied. Slowly he handed her his gift: a set of tortoise-shell combs with jeweled edges for her lovely hair—bought with the money he had received for selling his watch. Real love cannot think of any other way to give except to give lavishly, joyfully, and sacrificially.

David, in describing his love for God said, "I will not sacrifice to the LORD my God burnt offerings that cost me nothing" (2 Samuel 24:24). Love does not give leftovers. Love gives what is most costly and discounts the consequences.

The broken flask is a symbol of the kind of person God uses. Elisabeth Elliot describes suffering as "having something you don't want, or wanting something you don't have." This could apply to anything that causes us to suffer. Just as flowers give off a stronger fragrance when they are crushed, so our devotion is deepened by the trials we have endured and the grace we have received.

No wonder commentators often see here a further meaning. In this story, we see a picture of the church, filled with the beautiful fragrance of devotion because of Mary's selfless deed. "A lovely deed brings into the world something permanently precious, something which time can never take away."[2]

We want a religion that is positive, light, and cheery; we do not like to be challenged with the depth of devotion that is needed to please Jesus and make an impact in the world. Sometimes crushing is the route to greatness. Just ask Job, Paul, or even Jesus, who had to learn "obedience from what he suffered"

(Hebrews 5:8). There is probably no one whom God greatly uses that hasn't first been broken and humbled.

Jesus asked, "Why do you criticize her excessive generosity?" The question should not be why was this woman willing to "waste" all of this expensive perfume, but why we ourselves do not readily have comparable examples of extravagant love in our own day and culture. Unfortunately, we are taught only to give rationally and in calculated amounts. But Jesus has even a greater claim on us than helping the poor.

Everyone has a different idea as to how money should be spent, and sometimes the disagreement is legitimate. If you spend it for the poor, how should it be distributed? And if you choose to build an orphanage, who draws the line between adequate and extravagant? And if you want to support missionary endeavors, where do you get the "biggest bang" for your buck? But we'd all agree that pouring a flask of expensive perfume on a man condemned to die appears at first blush to be an obvious waste.

Love is glad to waste. Love sometimes does spontaneous and outrageous things. Sometimes it takes what has been saved for other purposes and squanders it on the one who is loved. The heart does not always follow the head. Love caused the father of the prodigal to welcome his son home, the very one who had insulted him by asking for his inheritance early and then tarnished the family name.

"Jesus Christ has erected a memorial to this good woman more lasting than brass, more enduring than marble, which will still exist when the proud monuments of earth have perished, when the pyramids of Egypt shall have mingled with the sands of the desert."[3] This monument is greater than Lady Liberty, who welcomes immigrants at New York's harbor. Mary's pedestal is the whole earth, for wherever the gospel is preached, her story will be told. There would always be opportunities to help the poor, but there would be only this *one* opportunity to anoint Jesus for His death and burial. What she did was worth remembering.

Mary knew that nothing was too costly to give to Jesus. Hadn't He given her the priceless gift of forgiveness? More than all the men who watched and complained about her extravagance, she understood that she was in the presence of the One who deserved her highest praise and worship. She did something none of them would dare to do. There was no regret for the practical financial loss. Only the regret that there was not more to give.

THE MESSAGE OF RESURRECTION
Not only has the fragrance of Mary's perfume filled the world, but it also instructs the world.

What message did she leave us?

First, a message of resurrection. The Bible doesn't say that Mary actually knew Jesus was going to shortly be put to death and buried. But the clear statement of Jesus, "It was intended that she should save this perfume for the day of my burial" (John 12:7), implies that she *kept* this perfume, with the *intention* that it be used for His burial. In those days it was customary that the dead body of a loved one be anointed. Mary of Bethany did it while He was alive, rather than waiting until He died. This was one of the last acts of kindness Jesus experienced. She understood what others did not.

How did Mary know? No doubt she knew because she had paid close attention as the Master spoke. She was the one who sat at His feet and heard His Word. Jesus, for some time, had been speaking of His burial, expecting the disciples to understand, but they did not. Peter reproached Him, and the other disciples also believed that His death was inconsistent with His mission. Even after His death, the disciples were slow to believe in the Resurrection.

But Mary understood.

Interestingly, Mary of Bethany is not mentioned as going to the tomb on Easter morning with the intention of embalming the body. She had given her gift while He was alive and saw no need to do it later. Of course we commend the other women who brought the spices intending to give their Savior a proper burial. But this Mary—bless her—had *already* anointed him.

This might also give us a further explanation for her unbound hair. The Jews when in grief and mourning made themselves unkempt in appearance, and Mary would follow the custom of the day. "She knew that she was anointing her great Teacher for burial, that her lavish gift would cling to Him on the cross and in the tomb. Her disheveled hair was in keeping with her mourning spirit."[4]

A father in a funeral home here in Chicago wrote a note and put it under the hand of his dead son who lay in a coffin. The words said simply, "I love you." How much better to say those words when the boy was alive? How much better to give flowers when our loved ones can appreciate them rather than to wait until they surround the casket?

Second, she preached a message of grace. Her deed of kindness would be an inspiration to our broken world. Her devotion to Jesus cost her something that was valued, but in return, she blessed generations she would never meet. She reminds us that the grace that comes to us through Jesus is not only worth our personal devotion, but it is also a message we must bring to the world. "Every time we love, we increase our capacity to be hurt. But the New Testament church won the world because they out-loved everyone else."[5]

One act of love can change a child, or a marriage, or a church. There are hidden dominoes of blessing that we cannot see, but that go on even to eternity.

TRANSFORMING LESSONS

Love does not count the cost. If you love Jesus, you are willing to be misunderstood, you are willing to take risks, you are willing to leave all and follow Him, you are willing to turn down a high paying job in favor of serving underpaid and underappreciated in a foreign country. Why? Because *love for Jesus trumps other priorities.*

Mary teaches us a lesson of extravagant waste. The broken vessel was poured over the broken body. The apostle Paul, in going over the instructions for the Lord's Supper with the Corinthian church mentions the scene from the Last Supper where Jesus breaks the bread. "This is my body, which is broken for you: this do in remembrance of me" (1 Corinthians 11:24, KJV). Jesus knows what it is like to be broken; His life was poured out for us so that through this demonstration of love He could offer us forgiveness. "He was wounded for our transgressions, he was bruised for our iniquities" (Isaiah 53:5, KJV). His brokenness is the basis of our own redemption.

Contrast Mary with the stinginess of Judas. Interestingly, Judas said this gift was a *waste.* Yet, Jesus later applied the same Greek word to Judas himself, when in His prayer to the Father He said, "None has been lost except the one doomed to destruction so that Scripture would be fulfilled" (John 17:12). That word *destruction* is the same word translated *waste* in this passage.

So, Judas criticized Mary for "wasting" money, but he wasted his entire life. Mary gave her best in love and devotion; Judas gave his worst in selfishness and rebellion. He solved the problem of how the Jewish leaders could arrest Jesus without causing a riot at the feast. He sold Jesus for the price of a slave. In the presence of Jesus, his heart became harder, not softer.

Finally, nothing done for Christ is wasted. Paul says that the financial support that was given to him is a "fragrant offering, an acceptable sacrifice, pleasing to God" (Philippians 4:18). The fragrance of our gifts and good deeds passes away, but it is ever present to Jesus.

As a result of Mary's devotion, the house was blessed with the fragrance. The village itself was blessed, as it is famous today as the town of Mary and Martha and Lazarus. And the world is blessed as the fragrance of her worship reaches us in our hectic and ungrateful culture. And of course, *Jesus* was blessed.

A few years ago, Karen, the wife of one of our pastors joined a group of people traveling to Namibia, Africa, to bring clothing and food to the starving people in the Osiree refugee camp. She was shocked at the desperate conditions these people were living in—parents starving themselves so that their children could have their food. Yet, Christians had joy despite their suffering. One night, as she heard rats scurrying around the floor of the tent, God called her to help these people. Since that first trip, she has made more than ten trips to Osiree, taking others with her; she has motivated our church to build a women's center and a church building for the believers; she has taught the women different skills, including how to quilt; and has organized enough clothing, food, medical supplies, and equipment to fill five semitruck containers that have been sent to the refugee camp. Karen's single-minded devotion to Christ has brought hope and great blessing to thousands.

Years ago a man would walk down a street, lighting the lamps along a village pathway. At dusk you could not see the lamplighter, but you could tell where he had been by the lights he left behind. Just so, we will pass on and no longer be seen on this earth, but others will see the good deeds we left behind. "Blessed are the dead who die in the Lord from now on. 'Yes,' says the Spirit, 'they will rest from their labor, for their deeds will follow them'" (Revelation 14:13). Like a stone thrown into a pond, the ripples go on to eternity.

Let us not resist the crushing that God brings into our lives. If flowers had not been crushed, Mary would not have had the perfume to give to Jesus. Just so, our Master crushes us that we might become His fragrance in our worship and service. We are broken by Him in order to win a world that is broken by sin. So our wisest investment is to lose our lives that we might gain them for the sake of the Kingdom. "Whoever finds his life will lose it, and whoever loses his life for my sake will find it" (Matthew 10:39).

Jesus calls us to that kind of devotion to win a broken world. Whatever we keep for ourselves is lost; whatever is given to Jesus remains. "Our most valuable possession, our costliest treasure should be laid at Jesus' feet."[6]

A PRAYER

Heavenly Father, give me the heart of Mary; let me be willing to love You with sacrifice and extravagance. Teach me the value of costly worship. Show me those things that I am yet holding back from Your control and purpose. With Your help, I am willing to be crushed by Your loving hand. I desire only one thing: to please You and give You a fragrance that will last for all of eternity. Please show me what sacrifice You want me to make for You. In Jesus' name, Amen.

After this, Jesus traveled about from one town and village to another, proclaiming the good news of the kingdom of God. The Twelve were with him, and also some women who had been cured of evil spirits and diseases: Mary (called Magdalene) from whom seven demons had come out; Joanna the wife of Cuza, the manager of Herod's household; Susanna; and many others. These women were helping to support them out of their own means.   LUKE 8:1-3

JESUS, MARY MAGDALENE, AND THE LEGENDS

"The marriage of Jesus and Mary Magdalene is part of the historical record," Dan Brown writes in his mega–best seller, *The Da Vinci Code*.[1] He is not the first to link Jesus and Mary together in holy matrimony. The book *Holy Blood, Holy Grail*, written by Michael Baigent, Richard Leigh, and Henry Lincoln, which Dan Brown credits for many of his ideas, expounded the same theme back in 1982.

Many women feel deeply about this matter, arguing that if the marriage of Jesus *did* happen and the truth was suppressed, then the full story must be told both to vindicate the reputation of Mary Magdalene and to prove that Jesus intended women to have equal authority in the church. Many books and television specials now are devoted to the relationship of Jesus and Mary.

Dan Brown says that it was Jesus' intention to build the church on Mary Magdalene, but power-hungry men stole it from her and gave the responsibility to Peter. When Mary Magdalene wept at the cross, she was not merely the wife of Jesus, but was pregnant with His child, Brown claims. For safety, she fled to Egypt and later to France, where her daughter Sarah married into the French line of Merovingian kings. Needless to say, some people are using Brown's theories to rewrite history and give Mary Magdalene an increasing role in the birth of the church.

Margaret Starbird, a devout Roman Catholic, is the author of *The Woman with the Alabaster Jar*. In that book, she argues that on the basis of what we might call historical probability, it is reasonable to suppose that Jesus was indeed the husband of Mary.

If this were true, why would the church keep this secret hidden from the general public? Why was the marriage of Jesus not included in the canonical Gospels? The answer, according to Starbird, is that such knowledge would have been a physical threat to Mary, so the details of their relationship were never included in the records. She goes on to say, "Of course I cannot prove that the tenets of the Grail heresy are true—that Jesus was married or that Mary Magdalene was the mother of his child. . . . But I *can* verify that these are the tenants of a heresy widely believed in the Middle Ages; that fossils of the heresy can be found in numerous works of art and literature; that it was vehemently attacked by the hierarchy of the established Church of Rome; and that it survived in spite of relentless persecution."[2]

The Da Vinci Code is so named because it says that Leonardo da Vinci belonged to a group called The Priory of Sion, an organization that was well aware of the marriage of Jesus and Mary. This exclusive club passed the secret from one generation to another with an elaborate ceremony. Leonardo, who was supposedly a member of the Priory, could not publicly tell what he knew since he would have incurred the bitter wrath of the church. So the master painter had to resort to encoding the heretical truths into his paintings.

Thus, in his famous painting, *The Last Supper*, Brown goes on, Da Vinci painted Mary Magdalene sitting next to Jesus; it is not John the apostle as generally believed. And there is no chalice on the table because Mary herself is the cup, the Holy Grail, because she bore the blood of Jesus by bearing His child. We are told that secret documents, if they were revealed, would verify these conclusions.

We should note in passing that most art historians insist that it is indeed John seated to the right of Christ, not Mary as *The Da Vinci Code*'s fictional account says. And there was no chalice on the table because Leonardo was interested in the betrayal, not the Eucharist. The idea that Mary is the chalice because she bore Jesus' child is a recent fictional development.

As you know, this alternate story of the beginning of Christianity is being widely explored in our age, particularity by those who insist that the early church was more accepting of women than in later centuries. The walls of some Roman catacombs show pictures of women with their hands raised in prayer, apparently assuming the role of a bishop. So some believe that if Mary could be shown to have been married to Jesus, this would verify the suspicions of some that Jesus was inclusive and that the church suppressed the truth to maintain male dominance and power.

The discovery of the Gnostic Gospels in 1945 opened up a whole new chapter in the discussion about Mary Magdalene. The Gnostics (based on the word *gnosis*, from which we get the word *knowledge*), lived just after the time of Jesus and claimed to have knowledge through esoteric experiences (that is, knowledge revealed only to a small group of the initiated). This *Gnosis*, as it was called, provided insights only available to those who were enlightened.

Their version of Christianity was, among other things, more pro-feminine than the early church of the New Testament. God is sometimes described as androgynous—that is, both male and female. Some of the Gnostic writings speak of sexual rituals, and others make convoluted reference to teachings about Jesus and His disciples. They believed that we could encounter Jesus by looking within ourselves, not looking to the records of objective history.

The early church fathers believed that the Gnostics were heretics who dismantled the authentic teachings of Jesus to justify their own theories of personal enlightenment. Scholars have long known the teachings of the Gnostics through the lens of the writings of these early church fathers who wrote against this widespread heresy. However, the actual documents of the Gnostics were lost, unknown to the world.

Then came a discovery in Nag Hammadi in Egypt in 1945, when the long-since buried documents were found. Understandably, they were of great interest to scholars and shed some valuable light on the early centuries of the church. Among the documents are various gospels attributed to the followers of Jesus; indeed, *The Gospel of Thomas* purports to contain 114 sayings of Jesus Himself.

What is the connection between these documents and Mary Magdalene? She is mentioned several times as being in close association with Jesus. In fact, Mary is presented as the favorite follower of Jesus, the one to whom He gave special attention. Thus, these documents *appear* to supply what has been lacking in our studies of the relationship of Jesus and Mary.

THE GNOSTIC GOSPELS

In *The Da Vinci Code* we are told that in concealing the truth about Jesus' marriage to Mary, the church has engaged in the "greatest cover-up in human history." So, let us consider the evidence for the marriage in the two most important documents outside of the New Testament that actually speak of Jesus and Mary. First, in the *Gospel of Philip* we read:

> The companion is Mary of Magdala. Jesus loved her more than his students. He kissed her often on her face, more

than all his students, and they said, "Why do you love her more than us?" The savior answered, saying to them, "Why do I not love you like her? If a blind man and one who sees are together in darkness, they are the same. When light comes, the one who sees will see light. The blind man stays in darkness."[3]

You should know that because of the poor quality of the papyrus, a word or two is missing. The text reads, "Jesus kissed her often on the[blank]. . . ." So scholars fill in the blank with the word *mouth, face, forehead*, etc. Actually, for all we know the text might have said "the hand" or even "the cheek," since the statement implies that He also kissed His other students—presumably on the cheek as is customary in the Middle East.

That Jesus is presented here as the companion of Mary is perhaps the best evidence that exists for their supposed marriage. However, the word *companion* does not mean spouse, but rather sister or simply *companion* as the Gnostic Bible translates it. There is no evidence that they were regarded as husband and wife.

Is this account as it stands credible? Before we answer, we should remind ourselves that scholars believe this book was written in about the middle of the third century, about two hundred years after the time of Jesus—not exactly an eyewitness account. Whose description of George Washington would you more readily believe: the accounts of those who actually knew him and lived with him, or the description of someone who lived two hundred years after George Washington, especially if you knew that this later writer wanted to put his own political ideas into George Washington's mouth?

In the rest of *The Gospel of Philip*, Jesus is presented as one among many beings that emanated from God. These kinds of texts are clearly intended to articulate a pagan philosophy, not to write something credible about Jesus. You can write anything you want if you are not concerned about historical facts.

We don't have a clue as to who wrote this gospel. Most assuredly, it was not written by the Philip of the New Testament, but rather by some pseudoauthor who cobbled together a plethora of disjoined Gnostic ideas. The Gnostic writers used the names of the apostles to give their writings credibility. Perhaps this unknown author wrote what he did because legends about Mary Magdalene were already circulating by the third century. At any rate, this writer had an agenda and tried to use whatever means necessary to get it accomplished.

In another Gnostic book called *The Gospel of Mary*, Mary Magdalene is described as having a special revelation given to her by the Savior. At Peter's request, she tells the other disciples about a vision she had with Jesus and how she questioned Him about whether one sees a vision through the soul or through the spirit. The Savior answered, "A person sees neither through the soul nor the spirit. The mind, which lives between the two, sees the vision. . . ."

After some rather obscure explanations about the soul, Peter asks, "Did He really speak to a woman secretly, without our knowledge and not openly? Are we to turn and all listen to her? Did He prefer her to us?" Mary begins to weep and assures Peter that she did not make this up.

At this point, Levi steps into the conversation and says, "Peter, you are always angry. Now I see you contending against this woman as if against an adversary. If the Savior made her worthy, how are you to reject her? Surely the Savior knows her very well. That is why He loved her more than us."[4] Then the disciples are admonished to go out and preach, which they do.

I believe this account is another attempt of the Gnostics to give legitimacy to their esoteric doctrines of knowledge for the inner circle of the initiated. This account was likely included for two reasons: first to make the point that women should be able to preach, and second and most importantly, that private revelations from God have the same status as the teachings of bishops. Mary Magdalene, who figures prominently in the Gospels, as the first witness to the resurrection would be the natural person to be chosen for the dialogue.

Although we have every reason to reject the accounts given in these two Gnostic Gospels, we should note that even if they were accurate, it is a stretch to say that they point to a romantic relationship between Mary and Jesus, much less marriage. At this point, as in so many others, *The Da Vinci Code* bases its conclusions on imaginary data, hoping that gullible readers will give credence to these tales.

THE LEGENDS

In my (Erwin) study of this subject, I took the time to read *The Templar Revelation* by Lynn Picknett and Clive Prince, a book that argues in detail that Jesus and Mary were married, or at least that they were sexual partners. In brief, the authors toured the Magdalene shrines of southern France where legends about Mary arose in about the ninth century. The purpose of their book is to evaluate this folklore and argue for its plausibility and, in the process, to attempt to destroy the traditional teaching about Jesus as found in the New Testament.

In their travels, the authors discovered that legends about Mary Magdalene are linked with the pagan goddess Isis and the mother-child cult associated with Mary, the mother of Jesus. What is more, wherever there are Magdalene centers, there are also shrines and myths about John the Baptist. The authors argue that John actually did not put himself under the authority of Jesus as the New Testament claims; rather that Jesus was a disciple of John. And John's anointed successor was actually the Gnostic sex magician Simon Magnus, who is mentioned in the book of Acts.

If you've still not heard enough, it might be a surprise to learn from *The Templar Revelation* that Jesus, John the Baptist, and Mary Magdalene all had "Gnostic awareness of the Divine," baptizing people and thus initiating them into "the ancient occult tradition." The miracles of Simon Magnus, like those of Jesus, were an intrinsic part of this religious practice. "Ritual was central to this movement, from the first baptism to the enactment of the Egyptian mysteries. But the supreme initiation came through sexual ecstasy."[5]

If you are wondering where all of this comes from, understand that the basic method of the authors is this: they take all of the legends and occult practices of ancient times and interpret the New Testament accounts in light of these esoteric mythologies. That is, they force the New Testament stories to fit pagan myth and rituals. Thus, we should not be surprised that Jesus Himself turns out to be the son of a goddess, and the anointing by Mary of Bethany (the authors believe she is Mary Magdalene) turns out to be a sexual ritual performed by a priestess. "The anointing of Jesus was a pagan ritual: the woman who performed it—Mary of Bethany—was a priestess. Given this new scenario it is more than likely that her role in Jesus' inner circle was as a sexual initiatrix."[6]

Christians should be appalled by these allegations. But once mythologies are given the status of history and imaginary connections are made between seemingly related events, any spin can be imposed upon the records of the past. And then, one can go on to say that the reason the real "truth" was banned from the Bible is that the church has always championed sexual repression and the degrading of women. The power-hungry, money-loving church has always stood in favor of male supremacy, rigid control, and the rejection of "the divine feminine."

How incredible that occult writers should so twist the New Testament as to make it an occult document. The very writings that call us to a life of holiness and purity are pressed into service to affirm an immoral pagan agenda. Imagine the Jesus who said, "anyone who looks at a woman lustfully has already committed adultery with her in his heart"—imagine this Jesus approving and evidently participating in an occult sex ritual.

We can understand why Irenaeus (AD 130–200), commenting about how the Gnostics used the Bible in his day, said that it is like taking a beautiful picture of a king and reassembling it to become a picture of a fox. No wonder Peter, speaking of false teachers, wrote, "Many will follow their shameful ways and will bring the way of truth into disrepute. In their greed these teachers will exploit you with stories they have made up" (2 Peter 2:2-3). As it was then, so it is today!

FURTHER EVALUATIONS

We often hear it said that the early church regarded Mary Magdalene as the "apostle of the apostles." This is not explicitly stated in an ancient text, but it is implied by Hippoytus, a third-century leader who did regard women as apostles. In his commentary on The Song of Solomon, he writes, "Lest the female apostles doubt the angels, Christ himself came to them so that the women would be apostles of Christ and by their obedience rectify the sin of ancient Eve. . . . Christ showed himself to the (male) apostles and said to them: . . . 'It is I who appeared to these women and I who wanted to send them to you as apostles.'"[7]

It is worth noting that Mary is not singled out by name as an apostle, although she would be included in the statement about the women being apostles. This refers then to all the women who followed Jesus and were witnesses to the empty tomb. Hippoytus can, of course, call these women apostles, but we must remember his personal opinion should not be given the weight of canonical Scripture.

Interestingly, *The Da Vinci Code* says that "the winners write history," implying that the writers of the New Testament Gospels were agenda driven, and thus they covered up the facts they disliked and espoused only what the male leadership wanted to reveal. But these same modern scholars accept what the authors of the Gnostic Gospels say at face value, as if the Gnostics who lived well after the time of Jesus and wrote under false pretenses, were more reliable. Even if we say that the Gnostics were not the "winners," they were willing to sacrifice their integrity in order to get a wider hearing.

If we had time to compare the authenticity of the New Testament with that of the Gnostic Gospels we would soon see that the evidence for the reliability of the New Testament is compelling. In contrast, the Gnostic Gospels do not purport to be a history of Jesus or a history of anything else for that matter. They are esoteric documents, discussing religious experiences, not confirmable events of history. It is beyond credulity that some writers want to exalt the Gnostic Gospels at the expense of the historically verifiable New Testament accounts.

Are there other reasons given to accept the marriage of Jesus and Mary? Margaret Starbird argues that Jewish custom would necessitate that as a rabbi, Jesus would be married. However, we must realize that Jesus was not technically a rabbi, nor did He portray Himself as one. As Bock points out, the apostles called Him rabbi because He was their teacher, but He did not have an official role in the Judaistic structure of the day. This explains why the Jews asked Jesus by what authority He did certain things; He did not occupy any official position and He had no recognized role within Judaism.[8]

In addition, Jesus commended those who were called to be eunuchs, those unmarried for the sake of the Kingdom of Heaven. So regardless of the expectations of the day, Jesus most assuredly would not have felt the need to be married in order to accomplish His mission.

In 1 Corinthians 9:4-6, Paul argued that he has a right to have a wife. If Jesus had been married, we would have expected Paul to mention that and thus clinch his argument. But of course he did not do so, for there was no evidence that Jesus was married. Paul's words, however, do show (contrary to some writers) that the church was not embarrassed to reveal that its leaders were married.

Finally, as Bock points out, Jesus showed no special concern for Mary Magdalene at the cross. If she had been His wife and pregnant with His child, we would expect some reference to her from His lips. The bottom line? There were good religious reasons why some Jewish men did not marry, and others remained celibate for practical reasons. We simply cannot argue that Jesus was married based on ambiguous and slender cultural inferences.

We should note in passing that Mary Magdalene was never tied to any male; usually women were identified either by a husband or a brother. There are twelve references to Mary Magdalene in Scripture, and she is always mentioned singly, while other women are identified by their husbands. Mary Magdalene's name always stands alone.

Obviously if Jesus had been married to Mary Magdalene, this would have been the very kind of information that would have been exploited by Jesus' early followers. Craig Blomberg in *The Denver Journal* refers to the emphasis of Mary, the mother of Jesus, in the Roman Catholic Church, and then writes:

I would add also that with the very early veneration of Mary, the mother of Jesus, in Roman Catholicism, largely out of a desire to have a quasi-divine female figure along with God the Father, had Jesus ever been married such a woman could scarcely have disappeared with a historical trace. She would have been celebrated and venerated instead, especially in the very strands of Catholicism that *The Da Vinci Code* pits against the revelation of "the truth" of Jesus' marriage.[9]

Legends about Jesus and Mary can be traced back to the ninth century in France. One legend says that Mary and Sarah (the daughter of Jesus) came to southern France in a boat without oars. Some of these myths were incorporated into *The Da Vinci Code* with the pretense that they could have historical reliability. But we cannot build history on legends, nor can we build a case for a marriage on secret documents whose contents have never been revealed and whose whereabouts are unknown.

A QUESTION OF INTERPRETATION?

While purchasing a book at a popular bookstore, a clerk was overheard to say to a customer, "We all have different interpretations as to whether Jesus was married." The clear implication is that history is like putty, capable of being shaped into any mold we desire. Some people want Jesus to have been married and construct scenarios they say give evidence for it. Others point out that it is an inference without textual support. In other words, it appears that these questions cannot be settled, but are a matter of personal interpretation.

Not so.

The study of history is the examination of documents and artifacts. It cannot degenerate into an arbitrary decision to give myths the status of history. In her book, Starbird says that "where there is smoke there is fire," implying that since these myths about Jesus and Mary exist, it must mean that they have a basis in fact. Thus, myths about Jesus that surfaced nine hundred years after He was on earth are given credibility and status.

But mythology is exactly what it is—it is the study of myths that are either concocted to explain various phenomena (such as the Greek and Roman myths) or invented to give credibility to an event or region. It is not hard to understand why in the ninth century, the St. Marie Delmar Church in southern France would latch onto a myth that Mary Magdalene and her daughter visited their shores. In an age prone to superstition, it is understandable that the most outlandish hearsay can be spoken of as factual. This also explains the superstitions in the same region about a visit from John the Baptist.

Given the dramatic story of Mary at the tomb of Jesus and His command that she tell the brethren about His resurrection, it is easy to see why she would be a candidate for the mythology that grew up about her. Myths also exist about her having gone to England, and some say she died in Egypt. In the absence of documentation, myths can spring up in any context and for any reason. But as a matter of principle, it is always dangerous to create a theory where factual evidence is lacking.

Much of modern scholarship proceeds on the premise that we should interpret the New Testament as if it were part of the paganism in which the ancient world was steeped. Thus, there are even attempts to make parallels between Mary Magdalene and Jesus and the Egyptian god Isis and Cyrus. But we must study the New Testament on its own terms, remembering that it repudiates the paganism of the day and is not part and parcel with it. To understand the New Testament is to understand why paganism cannot be imposed upon it.

We do not have to rewrite the New Testament in order to find a proper respect for women within the early church. We do not have to say that Jesus was married to Mary Magdalene to give women their proper role within our faith communities. As this book has shown, Jesus elevated the role of women and regarded them as partners in His earthly ministry. He affirmed that women could appear in public and speak of His grace and power. He established their worth, dignity, and significance.

JESUS AND MARRIAGE

Could Jesus have been married?

Even if there is no evidence that Jesus was married, we still can speculate about whether or not He *could* have been joined to a woman in such an intimate relationship. As a man, we can assume that He would have desired such intimacy and companionship. And since marriage is "honorable and undefiled," we might be tempted to take the next step and say that yes, He could have been married.

However, since He had both a human and a divine nature, we must confess that it is unthinkable that Jesus, with a holy and divine nature, could be joined to a sinner in the most intimate, physical human bond. If He had married, presumably it would have been to someone as holy as He—which severely limited His options.

Of course, someday Jesus *will* be married. We all anticipate his future wedding. He is now engaged to us, the church—His bride. He would not have been married on earth knowing that His coming marriage is in heaven. He is not a polygamist. He is not married to each of us individually, but to all of us collectively, each a member of His one bride.

On that day, we, along with Mary Magdalene, will be invited to the Marriage Supper of the Lamb, where the marriage is consummated, not in a physical, sexual union, but in the most blessed, intimate union of fellowship imaginable. Yes, Jesus will be married—not to an individual woman, but to all of us who constitute the bride of Christ.

> "Let us rejoice and be glad and give him glory! For the wedding of the Lamb has come, and his bride has made herself ready. Fine linen, bright and clean, was given her to wear." [Fine linen stands for the righteous acts of the saints.] Then the angel said to me, "Write: Blessed are those who are invited to the wedding supper of the Lamb!" (Revelation 19:7-9)

Given this larger perspective, Jesus' obvious celibacy was both necessary and proper.

The invitation to attend this wedding does not come from the Gnostic Jesus, but rather from the Jesus who is King of kings and Lord of lords. "Therefore God exalted him to the highest place and gave him the name that is above every name, that at the name of Jesus every knee should bow, in heaven and on earth and under the earth, and every tongue confess that Jesus Christ is Lord, to the glory of God the Father" (Philippians 2:9-11).

Only those who accept His invitation will gather to enjoy the feast!

A PRAYER

Father, I thank You that Jesus has made me worthy to be called His bride. I pray that I might anticipate His marriage supper with the same enthusiasm as a wedding here on earth. Help me to be faithful to Him and not be caught up with competing lovers. For Jesus' sake, Amen.

ENDNOTES

Introduction

[1] Dan Brown, *The Da Vinci Code* (New York: Doubleday, 2003), 248.

Chapter 1

[1] M. Madeline Southard, *The Attitude of Jesus Toward Women* (New York: George H. Doran Company, 1927), 133.

[2] William Barker, *Personalities Around Jesus* (New Jersey: Fleming H. Revell, 1963), 96.

[3] Darrell L. Bock, *Breaking the Da Vinci Code* (Nashville: Nelson Books, 2004), 138.

[4] Leonard Swindler, "Jesus Was a Feminist," *Catholic World* (1971): 180.

[5] Quoted in Southard, *The Attitude of Jesus Toward Women*, 122.

Chapter 2

[1] Darrell L. Bock, *Breaking the Da Vinci Code* (Nashville: Nelson Books, 2004), 54.

[2] Mary Whelchel, unpublished manuscript.

[3] Ibid.

[4] William Barclay, *The Gospel of Mark* (Edinburgh: St. Andrews Press, 1955), 140.

[5] Augustine, Confessions, 1:1, translated by John K. Ryan (New York: Image Book, 1960). See web site last accessed October 17, 2005, http://www.amazon.com/gp/reader/0385029551/ref=sib_rdr_ex/002-6041383-9975243?%5Fencoding=UTF8&p=S018&j=0#reader-page

[6] M. Madeline Southard, *The Attitude of Jesus Toward Women* (New York: George H. Doran Company, 1927), 89.

[7] Barclay, *The Gospel of Mark*, 155.

[8] Southard, *The Attitude of Jesus Toward Women*, 88.

[9] William Barker, *Personalities Around Jesus* (New Jersey: Fleming H. Revell, 1963), 80.

Chapter 3

[1] *The MacArthur New Testament Commentary* Matthew 8–15 (Chicago: Moody Press, 1987), 467.

[2] Ibid., 474.

[3] Bonnie Thurston, *Women in the New Testament* (New York: The Crossroad Publishing Co., 1998), 73.

[4] Warren Wiersbe, *The Bible Exposition Commentary*, Vol. 1 (Wheaton, IL: Victor Books, 1989), 54.

Chapter 4

[1] William Barker, *Personalities Around Jesus* (New Jersey: Fleming H. Revell, 1963), 142.

[2] Ibid., 102.

Chapter 5

[1] Lydia Brownback, *Legacy of Faith* (New Jersey: P&R Publishing, 2002), xiii.

[2] Bonnie Thurston, *Women in the New Testament* (New York: The Crossroad Publishing Co., 1998), 71.

[3] Alicia Craig Faxon, *Women and Jesus* (Philadelpia: The United Church Press, 1973), 51.

[4] Liz Curtis Higgs, *Really Bad Girls of the Bible* (Colorado Springs: Waterbrook, 2000), 246.

[5] Warren Wiersbe, *The Bible Exposition Commentary*, Vol. I, Mark (Wheaton, IL: Victor Books, 1992), 127.

[6] William Barclay, *The Gospel of Mark* (Edinburgh: St. Andrews Press, 1955), 137.

Chapter 6

[1] William Barclay, *The Gospel of John,* Vol. 2 (Edinburgh: St. Andrews Press, 1955), 3.

[2] David Thomas, *Gospel of John* (Grand Rapids: Kregel Publications, 1980), 219.

[3] Barclay, *The Gospel of John*, 9.

[4] Thomas, *Gospel of John,* 220.

[5] Ibid.

Chapter 7

[1] Frank Minirth, Don Hawkins, and Roy Vogel, *Just Like Us—15 Biblical Stories with Take-Away Messages You Can Use in Your Life* (Jossey-Bass: A Wiley Imprint, 2004), 157.

[2] Ibid.

[3] William Barker, *Personalities Around Jesus* (New Jersey: Fleming H. Revell, 1963), 107.

[4] Ibid.

[5] Richard C. Lenski, *The Interpretation of St. Luke's Gospel* (Minneapolis: Augsburg Publishing House, 1946), 612.

[6] Minirth, Hawkins, and Vogel, *Just Like Us*, 161.

[7] Barker, *Personalities Around Jesus*, 109.

[8] Ibid.

[9] Joanna Weaver, *Having a Mary Heart in a Martha World* (Colorado Springs: Waterbrook, 2002), 9.

[10] J. Hastings, ed., *The Great Texts of the Bible: Luke* (Edinburgh: T&T Clark, 1952), 230.

[11] Henry Scougal, *The Life of God in the Soul of Man* (Harrisonburg, VA: Sprinkle Publications, 1986), 72.

[12] Weaver, *Having a Mary Heart in a Martha World*, 9.

[13] Debi Stack, *Martha to the Max* as quoted in Minirth, Hawkins, Vogel, *Just like Us,*168.

Chapter 8

[1] Margaret Starbird, *The Woman with the Alabaster Jar* (Rochester, VT: Bear and Co., 1993), xxi.

[2] William Barclay, *The Gospel of John*, Vol. 2 (Edinburgh: St. Andrews Press, 1955), 129.

[3] Bryan Wharton, *Famous Women of the New Testament* (New York: E.B. Treat Publisher, 1890), 232.

[4] M. Madeline Southard, *The Attitude of Jesus Toward Woman* (New York: George H. Doran Company, 1927), 46.

[5] Alan Clason, "The Value of Broken Things," *Alliance Witness*, April 1, 1987.

[6] Ibid.

Chapter 9

[1] Dan Brown, *The Da Vinci Code* (New York: Doubleday), 245.

[2] Margaret Starbird, *The Woman with the Alabaster Jar* (Rochester, VT: Bear and Co., 1993), xxi

[3] Willis Barnstone and Marvin Meyer, *The Gnostic Bible* (Boston and London: Shambhala, 2003), 273.

[4] Ibid., 479–481.

[5] Lynn Picknett and Clive Prince, *The Templar Revelation: Secret Guardians of the True Identity of Christ* (New York: Touchstone Books, Simon & Schuster, 1998), 350.

[6] Ibid., 258.

[7] Darrell L. Bock, *Breaking the Da Vinci Code* (Nashville: Nelson Books, 2004), 20.

[8] Ibid., 37.

[9] Ibid., 26.

FREE DISCUSSION GUIDE!

A DISCUSSION GUIDE FOR
Jesus, Lover of a Woman's Soul
IS AVAILABLE AT

ChristianBookGuides.com

Da Vinci Didn't Convince Me

A mega best-selling book and a blockbuster 2006 motion picture have millions of people asking: What's the truth behind *The Da Vinci Code*?

Tyndale House Publishers has an arsenal of solid resources to equip you with the full truth about the accuracy of the Bible, Jesus' attitude toward women, and the story of Mary Magdalene.

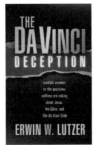

The Da Vinci Deception
Dr. Erwin Lutzer

A renowned expert's comprehensive, easy-to-read explanation of the truth behind the myths

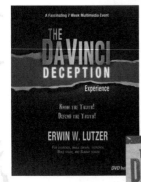

The Da Vinci Deception Experience
Dr. Erwin Lutzer

Based on Dr. Lutzer's popular book, an exciting multimedia event to equip your church, Bible study, or other group to defend the truth

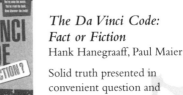

The Da Vinci Code: Fact or Fiction
Hank Hanegraaff, Paul Maier

Solid truth presented in convenient question and answer format

Jesus, Lover of a Woman's Soul
Dr. Erwin Lutzer, Rebecca Lutzer

The truth behind Jesus' relationships with and attitudes toward women, as seen through the eyes of those who knew him

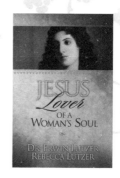

Magdelene
Angela Elwell Hunt

A captivating, biblically-based portrayal of the controversial life of Mary Magdalene

Maggie's Story
Dandi Daley Mackall

A contemporary fable that brings the story of Mary Magdalene to life for readers ages 15 to 19

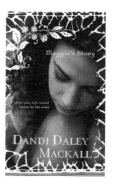

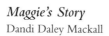

For more information, visit www.davincideception.com